ERNEST HEMINGWAY
FISHED HERE

BOOKS BY LARRY WAKEFIELD

All Our Yesterdays
a Narrative History of Traverse City and the Region

The Mystery of the Missing Nun

Historic Traverse City Houses
(with Lucille Wakefield)

Sail & Rail, A History of Transportation
(with Lucille Wakefield)

National Cherry Festival, An Illustrated History

Elmwood Township, An Illustrated History

Queen City of the North,
An Illustrated History of Traverse City

Butcher's Dozen, 13 Famous Michigan Murders

Traverse City Postcard History

Leelanau County Postcard History

Ghost Towns of Michigan (Vol. I)

Ghost Towns of Michigan (Vol. II)

Garfield Township, An Illustrated History

Grand Old Lady, An Illustrated History
of the Traverse City Opera House

ERNEST HEMINGWAY
FISHED HERE
And Other True North
Country Tales

Larry Wakefield
Illustrated by Dianne Wakefield

Published by Horizon Books
Traverse City, Michigan

ERNEST HEMINGWAY FISHED HERE

Printed in the United States of America by Horizon Books, Inc., 243 East Front Street, Traverse City, Michigan 49684.

FIRST EDITION

ISBN 0-915937-03-4

On the cover: Young Hemingway, 14, trout fishing in Horton Creek near Charlevoix, Michigan. *John F. Kennedy Library*. Cover design by Judy Albaugh.

for Philip and Jim

CONTENTS

ERNEST HEMINGWAY
FISHED HERE

A CHINA DOLL
FOR ABBIE

The village of Northport on Grand
Traverse Bay in Leelanau County was founded in 1854 by
Deacon Joseph Dame. In the spring of that year, with the
help of his son Eusebius, he platted the town on the shore of
the bay just north of Waukazooville, the Indian settlement
established five years earlier by his friend and colleague
Reverend George Nelson Smith. Waukazoo was the name
of the settlement's Indian chief.

The waters of Northport Bay, protected from all but
easterly winds, provided a safe anchorage, and Northport
soon became a regular port of call for ships that sailed the
Great Lakes on the Buffalo-Detroit-Chicago run: brigs, barks

1

and the swift, swallow-winged schooners, and later the wood-burning paddlewheelers and propellers that stopped regularly at Northport for fuel and supplies.

By 1860, Northport was a busy place–busier by far than Traverse City down the bay–but as yet only a handful of people lived there. Yet when the Civil War broke out, almost every able-bodied man in town was quick to answer Abraham Lincoln's call to arms. Northport, like most midwestern frontier towns, was fiercely loyal to the Union and the Republican party, and adamantly opposed to slavery.

One of the men to answer Father Abraham's call was young Bill Voice, son of "Uncle Billy," owner of the local sawmill. In the fall of 1862, along with 12 other Northport men, he joined a company of men from the Grand Traverse area recruited by Lieutenant Charles H. Holden for the 26th Michigan Infantry regiment. With pardonable pride and pugnacity they called themselves "The Lakeshore Tigers."

At 20, young Billy was the oldest of five children, three boys and two girls. The youngest was 4-year old Abigail or "Abbie," whom members of the family usually called "Did," on account of her spunky disposition– "I did!" she'd insist, "I did!" when one of her brothers teased her by accusing her falsely of skipping some duty or chore, for example.

The Voice family had come to Northport in 1853 from Traverse City, where "Uncle Billy," had built a sawmill for Perry Hannah. By 1855 he was operating a mill of his own at Northport.

Young Billy was the only boy in the family old enough to go to war. His family was proud of him, but little Abbie, who was his favorite, was heartsick. She idolized her big brother and couldn't bear to see him go. She wept bitterly on the evening of his departure.

In an attempt to comfort her, big brother Billy made a promise. "Don't cry, Did. Please don't cry," he said. "If you'll stop crying I'll bring you a real china doll when I come back."

But Abbie was inconsolable. She couldn't stop crying. She didn't want her brother Billy to go off to war. She was afraid something dreadful would happen to him. "Billy, don't go," she pleaded. "Please don't go."

And although she couldn't possibly have known it, she was right. Something dreadful did happen to Billy. From Northport the Lakeshore Tigers went south and into training camp at Jackson. And, just a few weeks later, Sergeant William H. Voice died of typhoid fever there–one of the diseases that killed twice as many men in the Civil War as died in battle.

On September 26, 1862, the steamer *Buffalo* docked at Northport on a grim and solemn mission. It carried the body of Billy Voice in a metal casket. Something strange was strapped to the top of it: a small wooden box. Inside the box Billy's family found a beautiful china doll. Even in death, Billy had kept his promise.

A detail of four soldiers had accompanied Billy's body home. When pressed with questions about the doll, they professed ignorance: they didn't know anything about it. Their orders were simply to see that the casket arrived safely at Northport and that the little box got there at the same time. They said they hadn't even known what was inside it. And so the real story of the doll remained a mystery.

It would be told eventually–but not for another 60 years.

Billy's funeral was held next day. It was attended by the largest gathering of people ever seen in Northport. The little log house that served both as school and church couldn't begin to hold all of them. They shared the family's grief. And all of them were intrigued by the story of the doll.

When people bought a ceramic doll in those days, they usually bought just the head and shoulders–the body would be made at home. After the funeral, several Northport women got together for a sewing bee and made a body for the doll and arms and legs, and then they sewed the clothing for it; a beautiful white silk dress and petticoat. Then they placed it in Abbie's arms, and she cried and said it was the most beautiful thing she'd ever seen and that she would keep it for the rest of her life. She named it Jeanette.

Abbie grew up and in 1878 she married her childhood sweetheart, Norman Morgan. He became one of Northport's most successful merchants. Later he built a hotel and advertised "free bus to the Bay View from the dock." He and Abbie were active in charitable work, particularly with the Northport Indians. They had grown up with the Indians, went to school with them, played with them, sang with them, loved them, understood their tragedy. Around the turn of the century, they sold their Northport interests and retired and moved down the Bay to Traverse City, where they continued their charitable activities.

It was shortly after World War I that Abbie learned about an old Civil War veteran who lived in a rooming house in her neighborhood. His name was Herman Dunkalow, and he had served in the 26th Michigan Infantry as a medical corpsman. Now, at age 90, the old man was sick and lonely. He needed someone to talk to, to visit with. All his family and his friends were dead.

That was enough for Abbie. With her kind and generous heart, she couldn't resist an appeal like that. She went to call on the old man. She found him in bed, too weak to get up, but eager to talk. Like many old soldiers Dunkalow liked to reminisce about his wartime experiences, and Abbie was a good listener.

Dunkalow said that it seemed to him that the young men in the Civil War were closer to their families than the soldiers of the World War. He remembered one man in particular–a young fellow was very sick and he kept raving about a doll, Dunkalow said. He begged everyone who stopped by his bed to get him a doll for his baby sister.

The doctors and nurses paid little heed to the young man's plea. They thought he was delirious. But Dunkalow was so touched that he went out and spent his last cent on a beautiful china doll with pink cheeks, brown eyes and black hair: Just the head and shoulders, he explained–that was all he could find in town.

Dunkalow said the young man grew calm and peaceful when he saw the doll. He asked Dunkalow to prop it up at the foot of the bed where he could see it. It was there when he died that night. Dunkalow said it was he who had seen to it that the doll be sent back to Northport with the young man's body. He had seemed so intense and determined about getting a doll for his sister, Dunkalow thought–maybe it wasn't just the raving of a dying man, after all.

Abbie had followed the old man's story with growing wonder and excitement. She could hardly wait for him to finish. Then she asked, "Do you remember the young man's name?"

"His name was William Voice," the old man said.

Abbie was trembling with emotion. She excused herself, saying she had an errand to run and would be back in a few minutes. She went home and got Jeanette from the dresser where she had kept her all those years, and hurried back to the old man's room. Holding the doll before him she said, "This is the doll you bought. And I am Bill Voice's little sister."

The old man could hardly believe his eyes. But he recognized the doll and knew her story must be true. His eyes filled with tears as he said:

"I'll never forget the look on your brother's face when he saw that doll." He paused, as though reflecting upon that hospital scene so long ago. Then he said, "I think your brother died a happy man."

5

THE
GREAT KNICKERS WAR

T he town was in an uproar. Especially
the women. There was talk of protest marches and threats of
a lynching party. The women were mad clean through. No
one could remember when they were all so angry and upset.

The object of their wrath was none other than Traverse
City's mayor, the Honorable Lafayette Swanton, Doctor of
Medicine. On or about June 1, 1922, the good doctor had
risen in righteous indignation and issued an order to Police
Chief John Blacken to arrest any woman who appeared on
downtown streets wearing knickers and behaving in an unladylike fashion.

In a public statement the mayor said: "Young men
and boys have been severely criticized for accosting women

on the streets, and I believe that much of this is because of the actions of the women."

He went on to say that women who "displayed their wares" and wore the "somewhat fashionable trimmings" might get in trouble with the authorities. He said he had checked this out with City Prosecutor Parm Gilbert, and Parm said, "Go ahead."

Asked who would decide on what was unladylike behavior, the mayor said, "Chief Blacken."

Asked what effect this might have on the tourist business, the mayor said he didn't know but that any tourist women who wore knickers downtown and behaved in that way could expect the same treatment.

The mayor went on to say he was also opposed to one-piece bathing suits. He knew that some women in Traverse City wore them, but he said their use was confined to cottagers who "staged their own beach parties" and did not mingle with the crowd on public beaches.

A storm broke over the mayor's head. Club women, factory workers, office girls, store clerks and high school girls— all announced plans to march down Front Street clad in knickers and carrying banners and signs of protest denouncing the mayor.

The mayor said he would fight this thing through to the end.

Next day the ladies got some powerful help from the Record-Eagle. In a front page column, the Observer (Editor Jay P. Smith) skewered Mayor Swanton on the barbs of his wit.

The column began:

Girls, you are safe!

You may wear your knickers

You may wear them right on Front Street.

The Mayor says so—BUT

You must not display your wares or any fashionable trimmings.

The Observer went on to say that he was at somewhat of a loss about what the mayor meant by "displaying your wares." The only wares he knew about were tinware, glassware, foot wear, underwear and the like. Perhaps the mayor meant legs. It was true that knickers reveal the legs but not so much as short skirts do.

As for "fashionable trimmings," did the mayor mean a frill or a flounce or a furbelow or pleating or a gathered hem on the bottom of the knickers?

The code should be defined so that the girls would be warned.

"Honestly, your honor," the Observer concluded, "there are bigger, more manly tasks awaiting your attention. How about improving the waterfront where city sewage pollutes the bathing beaches and perhaps the drinking supply. Take a walk down the alleys when the flies are breeding by millions and decide whether it's more important to eliminate the fly menace or dictate women's fashions."

W. J. Hobbs, secretary of the Chamber of Commerce, was more blunt in his denunciation.

"The Mayor is all wrong. His knickers campaign is absolutely ridiculous. Not only is it ridiculous, but it is damaging.

"My own daughter wears knickers and I wish my wife did. They are not only nice, modest and decent but they are pretty."

"Such a foolish campaign as this one against knickers is hurting everything and everybody. To what extent it will damage the tourist business will depend on the extent to which the news spreads. We know that the majority of the tourists wear them.

"To me it is much ado about nothing. This gets so d----d ridiculous that I think the whole city should rise and kill it right now."

It was already too late. The story had spread all over the Midwest; newspaper and wire services were clamoring for more knickers news stories. For once, the mayor had no comment. He could not be reached. He was digging in.

Two days later the turmoil came to a head. The lid blew off. To thoroughly mix the metaphors, a match was applied to the smoldering conflagration. What happened was that Mrs. Upsal Hobbs of Williamsburg, her daughter, Frances, and her daughter's girl friend, Eva Gaines, were ordered off Front Street by Chief Blacken. They refused to get off, and a little way down the street met Parm Gilbert, to whom they appealed the verdict. "Yes, get off," was Parm's reply.

Next morning Mrs. Hobbs issued a statement to the press. She said the girls had come to town directly from a school picnic at Williamsburg and had had no time to change clothes, as Mrs. Hobbs had some shopping to do.

"They were walking down the street, waiting for me to pick them up," Mrs. Hobbs explained. "Chief Blacken told them to get off the street. Then later we met Parm Gilbert, who said, 'Yes, get off!'

"My daughter and friend are fine girls," Mrs. Hobbs continued. "They are never out at night and always conduct themselves properly."

"If this is the way decent people are going to be treated in Traverse City, we will not come here any more. And we will see to it that other Williamsburg people don't come here either."

Clearly, things had gone too far. Now the merchants were up in arms. On behalf of people of Traverse City the Observer printed a public apology to Mrs. Hobbs and the girls. Parm Gilbert had second thoughts; he too made an apology.

"I went too far," the Prosecutor said. "I made a mistake and I acknowledge it. I offer my sincere apology."

Next day Mayor Swanton caved in. But not to the "Record-Eagle." He dropped in to the offices of the "Herald" in Grand Rapids and made a statement.

He claimed that he had been misquoted and misrepresented by a certain newspaper. Although he did not approve of knickers for street wear, he had issued no sweeping edict against them. His order was directed only against women who acted in an unbecoming manner. A particularly flagrant case was responsible for his instructions.

So ended the great knickers war.

Dr. Swanton appears to have been a courtly and kindly man. One must not judge him too harshly. In the context of his times he may not have been such a prude as it now seems.

In any case, the good doctor learned an important lesson the hard way. For the moral of the story is surely this: Any man who thinks he can tell a woman what she should or should not wear is obviously too big for his britches.

THE LOST
CHRISTMAS

Widow McGinnis was bone tired. With no hospital and only one doctor in town, she was literally run off her feet nursing the sick. Hardly had she finished one case than she was called out on another. She had spent the past week at Jack Fowle's boarding house nursing a young man named Marsh, who'd been hurt in an accident at the mill. But he was getting better now, and with Christmas just around the corner, she planned to take some time off and get rested up.

The Widow was a big-boned woman, heavy but not fat. She had plain strong features and kindly gray eyes that lit up her face. In winter she always wore a Scotch plaid cloak with a warm quilted hood that she had brought with her from Scotland. She spoke with a broad Scots accent.

Tomorrow was Christmas Day, and she was looking forward to seeing her son Jack. He worked in the woods but had been given a few days off to go home for Christmas. As a present she had knitted him a pair of double-yarn mittens, and she planned to get some soft leather from Patrick the Shoemaker to face them with before he went back to work.

Widow McGinnis lived in a little house in Slabtown, or, as some people called it, Baghdad. Except for Perry Hannah's cottage down the Bay—known as "The White House"—all the houses in Slabtown were made of slabs, edgings and other waste lumber from the mill.

The day had been cold, but clear and bright. But now, in the late afternoon, a northeast wind had come up and there were snowflakes in the air. From her west window the Widow could see the Bay — it looked dark and threatening.

Something brushed against her leg. It was Oliver, her cat and boon companion. Oliver was signalling hunger: it was suppertime. She had a fine dish of sausage on the shelf that Jack Fowle had given her, but she was saving it for Christmas dinner tomorrow, along with some pies she had baked. For herself, she'd as soon have good old "plum porritch," but Jack loved pie.

So she built a small fire in the cookstove and fried two slices of salt pork, one for herself and one for Oliver. She sliced some cold boiled potatoes into the hot fat and brewed herself a cup of tea. After the meal was over and the dishes washed and put away, she sat down to smoke her pipe and read her Bible by the light of the kerosene lamp.

Finally, it was bedtime. She donned her yellow flannel "bed-gown" and a linsey woolsey sack over it for extra warmth. Then she stoked the woodstove with a big chunk of maple, blew out the lamp and went to bed. She fell asleep listening to the snowflakes tapping softly at the window. It seemed like a big storm was in the making.

It turned out to be one of the biggest snowstorms in Traverse City history. It snowed hard all night, all Christmas Day and well into the night. The little village was buried. The snowdrifts in some places were 12 feet deep. Hardly anybody ventured out on Christmas Day. And the roads were so blocked with snow that nobody could get in or out of town. The lumberjacks had to spend Christmas in camp.

Next day, when the sun finally broke out people started digging out. Patrick the Shoemaker looked out and saw that the widow's little house was completely buried in the snow and there was no sign of life. But he wasn't worried—he thought she was still nursing the young man at Fowle's boarding house.

But then, one of the Norris boys, the two apprentices who lived with him—noticed a thin wisp of smoke rising from a hole in the snow above her smokestack. The widow was home after all, and perhaps she was in trouble. So they hastened to break out the shovels and excavated a path to her door.

Shoemaker Patrick rapped on the door, there was no answer. He rapped harder. "She must be in there," he said, and pounded on the door.

The racket finally roused her. She got up and groped her way through the dark room to the door, grumbling about people who'd "get a body out of bed this time of night."

Opening the door, she was blinded momentarily by the sunlight before she recognized her neighbors.

"Hoo!" she cried, marvelling. "The sun's up!"

"Up these past two hours, Mrs. McGinnis," said Patrick. "We worried about you being snowed in and all, so we took the liberty of digging you out."

"Now, that's very kind, Mr. Patrick," she said. "And a Merry Christmas to you all."

"Christmas?" he said. "Well, yes. But Christmas has come and gone, you know. It's the day after Christmas, this."

"Get along with you," said the widow, amiably. "Halloween's long gone. Tis na the time for playing tricks on poor auld souls."

But she invited them in for tea, and finally they were able to convince her that it was true. She had slept through Christmas. She had slept two nights and a day, 36 hours in all. Slowly she realized how it had happened. The snow covering her windows had made it so dark inside that when she got up from time to time to tend to the fire, she thought it was still night and went back to bed.

Slept through Christmas!

But somehow she didn't mind. Neither did she fret that Oliver had helped himself to the sausage. What was the poor creature to do? He might have starved otherwise.

Later that day, Perry Hannah having heard the news— it traveled from one end of the village to the other in no time— Perry Hannah himself sent his coachman with a sleigh, full of goodies: warm underclothing, a nicely browned chicken still warm from the oven, packages of tea and tobacco, and one of Mrs. Hannah's famous mince pies.

Slept through Christmas!

But Jack came home as soon as the roads were opened a few days later, and they had New Year's Day dinner together. By that time, the story of her long sleep had reached the lumber camps, too. Jack teased her about it, and they had a good laugh. And she presented him with the pair of double-yarn mittens, faced now with leather from Shoemaker Patrick. So what did it matter if Christmas was a few days late?

Slept through Christmas! Aye, but some good things had come of it, too, including this: The 36-hour sleep had left Widow McGinnis completely rested and restored, as good as new, ready and willing to take on those nursing jobs again.

So nothing important had been lost after all.

ERNEST HEMINGWAY
FISHED HERE

The best known of Ernest Hemingway's trout fishing trips in Michigan—immortalized in one of his greatest short stories, "Big Two-Hearted River"—took place in September of 1920. He and two friends took the train from Chicago to Seney, in Michigan's Upper Peninsula, and spent a week fishing the Fox River. The name of the river isn't mentioned in the story, only in the title, and that led to a great controversy among Hemingway aficionados about which river it was—the Fox or the Big Two-Hearted. Hemingway finally put the matter to rest in an essay entitled "The Art of the Short Story," which contains the following paragraph:

"The river was the Fox, by Seney, Michigan, not the Big Two-Hearted. The change of name was made purposely, not from ignorance nor carelessness, but because Big Two-Hearted River is poetry."

Perhaps the least known of his many fishing trips in Michigan was one he took with a Chicago friend, Lew Clarahan, in the late spring of 1916. On that cross-country trip by lake steamer, railroad and on foot, the two sixteen-year-old boys fished Bear Creek in Manistee County, the Boardman River near Traverse City, and the Rapid River near Kalkaska. Hemingway kept a diary on the trip.

On Saturday evening, June 10, they boarded a lake steamer (either the *Illinois* or the *Missouri*) for Frankfort, Mich. After disembarking there next day, they hiked or caught a ride or both (the diary isn't clear on this point) to Onekama, 18 miles south; then walked the Manistee & North-eastern railroad tracks 7 miles east to Bear Creek, where they made camp for the night. In his diary Hemingway describes the creek as clear running and about 50 feet wide, with many trout jumping. He mentions that he killed a water moccasin on the railroad tracks.

They got up early next morning and fished the stream with both worms and flies. Hemingway caught 4 trout, the biggest of which was 18 inches long. "Great fighters," he wrote. "Took 15 minutes to land the big one." They fished downstream in the afternoon and caught more trout and a grayling.

On Tuesday morning they broke camp and took the train to Walton Junction, where they had dinner. Walton, which had been known as "Hell" during lumbering days, was still a rough-and-tumble town. It was the junction of three railroads, Grand Rapids & Indiana, Manistee & North-eastern, and the Traverse City railroad, a branch of the GR&I. Hemingway called at the post office for his mail but found there was none, and arranged to have future mail forwarded to Kalkaska.

Hemingway commented that Walton "put the junk in Junction."

In the afternoon they took the Traverse City train to Mayfield, made camp on the Boardman River, and fished downstream. Hemingway wrote that the Boardman was "between 30 and 50 feet wide and fairly deep, with a devilish current." He says that Lew went up a small creek (probably Jaxon Creek) while he continued downstream on the big river. Afterwards they made a spruce-bough bed and slept well.

It began raining about two o'clock next morning, but after breakfast the boys "cut through the woods about two miles and fished downstream."

"Lew caught 2 nice rainbows and six brook trout," Hemingway wrote. "I only caught one brook. The rainbows fought gamely and broke water. Lew caught them both at an old lumber dam." This was the original Brown Bridge lumber dam; a new one was built on the site in 1921.

After a trout dinner at camp, the boys walked to Mayfield and bought some supplies at the general store.

"In the afternoon," Hemingway continued, "we fished at the old deserted broken lumber dam. Lew caught two suckers about two feet long — they gave us some sensation while we tho't they were trout. It rained all night and we dried our soaked clothes in front of a roaring fire. Had a good supper and slept well."

The Boardman, Hemingway declared, was some river.

On Thursday morning they broke camp and hiked into Mayfield.

"We said so long to some old folks that we traded the two suckers to for a quart of milk. The old woman smoked a pipe. The old man is 78 and the woman 85. They were delighted with the suckers."

The boys took the train back to Rugg, a little place on the Rapid River," Hemingway wrote. "It is a creek about the size of Horton's with many clear places and deep holes, also 2 nice dams — we fished from 4 to 5 and Lew caught 1 nice rainbow and 2 brook trout and I caught 3 rainbows. We camped on a high hill. There was an old water power dam out there in the wilderness run by a fellow from Chicago — he had a rainbow 20 inches long."

"Horton's" refers to Horton's Creek, which flows into Lake Charlevoix near the little town of Horton's Bay; it figures in several of Hemingway's Nick Adams stories. The creek was only four or five miles from the Hemingway summer cottage on Walloon Lake, where Hemingway had spent summer vacations since he was a year old; he no doubt had fished Horton's Creek many times as a small boy.

The little village of Rugg, six miles west of Kalkaska, got its start when the railroad line from Rapid City to Kalkaska came through in the late 1890s. It had a sawmill and a shingle mill and a big general store. The power dam on the river was established in 1904 to supply light and power to Kalkaska. The power plant shut down in 1919, but the dam, recently repaired, is still there, holding back the deep water of beautiful Rugg Pond.

On August 10, 1916, just four months after Hemingway and Clarahan had fished there, Naldo Yeoman's general store at Rugg burned to the ground while its proprietor was helping in the search for Fred Hill, who drowned while fishing in the river. At that time, Rugg had a population of about 20. Its original name, Mossback, was said to be a disdainful term used by lumberjacks to describe early settlers.

It rained Thursday night, but the boys got up early and lost no time getting into the river after breakfast. "Lew lost a whale of a rainbow just below the power plant," Hemingway wrote. "I caught 10 brook trout and Lew caught nine. I certainly was glad to get our mail at Kalkaska. Lew caught two trout that would weigh about a pound apiece. We got our dinner cooked (bacon) and were just starting to fry the big rainbows when a thunderstorm came up and we had to go into the tent. We took some dandy pictures on the Rapid River. It is white water about every 50 feet, and the trout bite freely and gamely. We just kept the big ones and threw the others back. We met a nice old mossback by the name of Tanner who used to own the store.

"The Rapid," Hemingway declared, "is the prettiest, fastest, best fishing stream I have ever tried."

Because their blankets were still "kind of wet," the boys fished all night in a "nifty pool" below the power house, and had good luck. Hemingway caught 5 rainbows and 7 or 8 brook trout. "Great fun fighting them in the dark in the deep, swift water. One rainbow I caught was a peach, about a pound. Lew caught several brooks."

Next morning, Lew went to sleep in the power house, which was electrically heated, and slept until eight o'clock, while Hemingway kept on fishing and caught several trout from the powerhouse window.

Later that morning they said goodbye to their Rugg friends.

"There were a lot of people who said they were sorry to see us go. We gave two nicely-floured trout to the grocery clerk and his wife at the store, and they wouldn't let us pay for any of the stuff we had ordered.

"The whole town came down to see us off," Hemingway said.

The boys hiked to Kalkaska and had a dinner at a "lumberjack joint." Then they parted, Clarahan by train to Frankfort on his journey home to Chicago, Hemingway north on the train to Mancelona and Petoskey, eventually to join his family at Walloon Lake.

The fishing trip provided Hemingway with background material for at least two of his Nick Adams stories: "The Battler," one of his best; and "The Light of the World," one of his weakest. (Hemingway said it was one of his favorites, but that nobody else liked it.)

In "The Battler" Nick meets a punch-drunk ex-prizefighter and his black companion in a hobo camp on Rapid River near the railroad tracks between Kalkaska and Mancelona. The chance encounter begins amicably but then turns ugly. Hemingway's model for Ad Francis, the battered old prizefighter, was lightweight champion Ad Wolgast, of Cadillac, Michigan.

In "The Light of the World," Nick and his friend Tom, while waiting for the train at the Kalkaska station become involved with six lumberjacks, four silent Indians, a lumbercamp cook, and two prostitutes. Tom is probably Lew Clarahan. Nick, of course, is Hemingway himself.

A LUMBERJACK
CHRISTMAS CAROL

Back in the days when pine lumber was king there lived in Traverse City a man named Sandy O'Donald, his wife Lizzie and their little boy Robbie. They lived in a little slab house on the west side of town near the Bay, in what was then called Slabtown or Baghdad. O'Donald worked in the sawmill during the summer and in the logging camps in winter. Among his peers in the lumber camps he was known as one of the best rivermen around.

O'Donald was a good worker and a good family man. He was a small, lean, quiet sort of man, of the kind that the Scots themselves call "dour"—and he never used two words when one would do.

His wife Lizzie was of a quite different disposition. She was gay, fun-loving and light-hearted, always singing at her work about the house, which she kept bright and spotlessly clean. She was several years younger than her husband. She was also very pretty, and the young men about town would often cast admiring glances upon her, which she neither encouraged nor disdained. But for all that, they seemed a happy and contented couple.

Then one day they were gone. People looked around and they were gone. They had packed up and departed without telling anyone where they were going or why . . .

Two years later, Sandy showed up at the sawmill with Robbie in hand. Together they walked into the office of the lumbercamp boss, Bill Rennie. He looked up from his desk and exclaimed:

"Sandy! Sandy O'Donald! Where on earth have you been?"

"Up at the Beavers," O'Donald said shortly.

"Where's Lizzie?"

"Lizzie's gone."

"Oh? Well, that too bad, too bad." The boss waited a moment to see if an explanation was forthcoming; then, knowing his man, he changed the subject. "Are you looking for work?"

"Aye," Sandy said. "That's why I'm here."

"Well, the Rennie Lake camp is starting up next month."

O'Donald hesitated. "There's just one thing," he said.

"And what might that be?"

O'Donald explained that he didn't want to leave his son Robbie behind. He had no one to care for him. Could he bring the boy to camp with him?

"You mean—to live?"

Sandy nodded, then said, "You could take his board out of my pay."

"Well, as far as that goes he wouldn't eat much, I'm

sure. But I don't know. I don't know how the men will take it. Maybe they'll all want to take their kids with them. Maybe we'd have to start up a nursery school."

"Doesn't seem likely," O'Donald said. Then he added, "He could make himself useful, earning his keep with small kitchen chores and such."

"Say no more," said Bill, unwilling to lose this man. "We will give it a try then. We will try it out and see if it works."

"I thank ye," said Sandy O'Donald.

So when October came around it found the boy and his father at the Rennie Lake camp together. The cook that year was a gentlemanly Englishman who took to Robbie from the start. He and his helper—who was only a few years older than Robbie—did what they could to keep him occupied and happy while his father was out in the woods.

And the men grew fond of him too, but they also felt sorry for him because he always looked so sad. He was quick to respond with a smile when spoken to, but in repose his face was sad. He had big brown eyes like his mother's (Sandy's were light blue) but by nature he seemed to take after his father.

In the late afternoon he would often sit by the window waiting and watching for the men to return, then rush into his father's arms when he came through the door. And from supper till bedtime they were always together, sitting side by side on the bunk bed while the father told him stories or sang to him in a low melodious voice. But Sandy would always bundle him off to bed early so that he might not hear any more of the lumberjack's strong language than was unavoidable.

But then a strange thing happened. Of their own accord the men began to moderate their usual coarse talk, to take some of the rough edges off their language. And sometimes when an oath or obscenity slipped out willy-nilly, the speaker would clap a hand sheepishly over his mouth and peek around to see if the boy had overheard.

Big Bill Rennie professed astonishment: "These ya-hoos are beginning to act like Sunday school teachers," he said. "Am I awake or dreaming?" But secretly he was pleased, too, for Robbie's sake.

As Christmas drew near, some of the men grumbled because the boss said he couldn't spare a single man off for the holiday—time enough for that, he said, when the most of cut was out. But he promised them an extra-special dinner, and hinted at other surprises. And then there were strange and secret preparations, and the supply wagons brought back mysterious packages from town—and some of the men were "in the know" and some were not, and the initiated ones would tell the uninitiated "Go mind your own business!" when they got too nosey.

Christmas Eve was the coldest that anyone could remember. Snow lay four and five feet deep in the silent woods. Every tree was weighted down with blankets of snow, and every stump had an overhanging mushroom-like white cap. Sleigh runners squeaked on the frozen roads, icicles hung from men's beards, frost sparkled on the coats of the oxen and the horses.

But inside the shanty all was of good cheer. The men came in early from the woods, and Big Bill was as good as his word: the dinner was turkey and all the trimmings. And after the tables were cleared and set back against the wall, Jim Value brought out his fiddle and one of the Micham boys his accordion, and two or three of the men got up and danced a jig while they played Nellie Bly, Old Dan Tucker and Hi, Betty Martin.

Meanwhile, something was going on behind a screen of blankets in one corner of the room, where the cook and two of the men had disappeared. Jack McGinnis was dancing a Highland fling in the grand manner when "Cookie" stuck his head out and gave the signal. The music stopped and the improvised "curtain" fell, revealing a beautiful Christmas tree lighted with candles and festooned with chains of popcorn and ribbons and striped candy canes and small wrapped gifts. Robbie, sitting on his father's lap, clapped his hands in delight.

But the climax was still to come. Suddenly Big Bill Rennie appeared dressed as Santa Claus, with a full white beard, stocking cap and an immense fur coat. Then there was so much laughter and cheers and stamping of feet that it seemed the shanty roof would be raised to the sky.

The tree at first had been planned only for Sandy's "kid," but as one after another of the men had been let into the secret, the chance to "come a drive" on someone was too good to lose. So while Robbie's lap was piled high with ingenious little hand-made toys, as well as "boughten" things like yellow-and-red jumping jacks, wooly sheep on wheels, bright red mittens and scarfs, and enough candy to make a dozen kids sick—each of the men found something on the tree for himself, something that pointed out his own particular foible or peculiarity.

Some of the jokes were pretty coarse, but all were taken in good humor, provoking much mirth and raillery.

So absorbed was everyone in the merry-making, and so noisy the festivities, that nobody heard the jingle of bells as a great sleigh-load of people, all muffled to the eyes, came dashing up, the splendid horses blowing plumes from their nostrils and steaming in the frosty air. The door burst open and the visitors trooped in, laughing and cheering—a jolly crowd of townspeople including some of the lumberman's wives, two or three young couples and tall Enoch, the driver.

Suddenly in the midst of all the hubbub, a shrill voice cried out:

"Daddy, Daddy, it's Mamma! Mamma's come back!"

And Robbie ran and clung to one of the women, whose white cloak had fallen from her head. She knelt and took him in her arms, but her wide brown eyes were fixed upon Sandy's blue.

"Have you come back then, lass?" he asked with a catch in his voice.

"Oh, Sandy," she said, "can you ever forgive me?"

And Sandy, for once loquacious, whispered, "Wheesht, lass. There's nowt to forgive. 'Twas me to blame more than yourself."

O, that was a wondrous Christmas, and no one there would ever forget it, when the stars shone softly down on the reunited family, as once they did on another little family in Bethlehem so many years ago.

THE NIGHT THE KLAN RODE INTO TRAVERSE CITY

On Saturday, August 9, 1924, in Traverse City was hot and humid: typical dog days weather.

The afternoon paper had stories about the Leopold-Loeb murder trial in Chicago, which was nearing mid-course; and the presidential campaign, which was heating up. (Democrat John Davis denounced the Ku Klux Klan, but his opponent, "Silent Cal" Coolidge, was mum on the subject.)

Mrs. George Spink, of Minnesota Junction, Wis., claimed that her health had been restored from almost complete disability by Lydia Pinkham's Vegetable Compound. Frank Smith, a former Traverse City businessman, was injured in an auto accident at 8th and Division. A "shivery, quivery" mystery thriller, "The Bedroom Window" with Meg McAvoy and Malcolm MacGregor, was playing at the Lyric Theatre. And as it turned cooler toward evening, a lot of people decided to go see it. In thrills, they got more than they bargained for.

At almost precisely the stroke of eight, with a full house and the main feature in full swing, a loud explosion rocked the building. It was followed immediately by two more in rapid succession. The first startled the people in the audience, the second brought them to their feet, and the third sent them scrambling in a mad dash for the exits.

Possible catastrophe was averted when a few of the cooler heads—notably manager Con Foster and his employees, and an off-duty fireman named Jim Baker—quickly took the situation in hand. Shouting "Sit down! Sit down!" and waving their arms and wrestling with the crowd, they finally succeeded in restoring order.

A few women had fainted and a few people were injured in the rush for the doors, but nobody was seriously hurt.

The explosion took place across the river behind the theatre, on open ground belonging to Jim Ott; he had a few piles of lumber standing there. Later, the police found three shallow depressions in the ground, each about six feet wide and six inches deep, where the charges had been set off. The blasts broke a lot of windows in the buildings along Front Street between Park and Cass—especially in the Elks building, the Sherman & Hunter clothing store, and a rooming house owned by Beulah Holliday —and rattled windows as far away as Sixteenth Street.

The stores downtown were full of Saturday night shoppers; they emptied quickly as people poured into the street to find out what was going on. Cars raced up and down the streets looking for the source of the bomb blasts and, for a while, all was confusion.

Adding to it was the sight of a huge flaming wooden

cross on the Ott property across the river. It burned until 10 o'clock that night, when the fire department made a run and put it out, for fear the fire would spread to the stacks of lumber nearby.

Meanwhile, a whole flock of fiery little crosses began springing up like mushrooms all over town. They were crude, makeshift affairs built of scrap lumber. About three feet high and two feet wide, they were nailed to blocks of wood and wrapped with oil-soaked rags.

Unidentified men in cars raced around town, planting crosses at every street intersection. They were followed closely by other cars, whose occupants set the crosses afire— sometimes, astonishingly, they were lighted by children who tumbled out, touched a match to the oily rags and scrambled back on board while the car was still in motion.

They, in turn, were followed some time later by fire-men on a tank-truck who doused the flaming crosses as fast as they could, though they were hard-put to keep up. Others were extinguished by people who dashed from their houses with buckets of water.

At Front and Wellington the cross had been thrown into the Boardman River by the time the fire truck arrived, and at corner of Franklin and State a little girl ran out and kicked one over. Still others were knocked down by passing motorists; one of them reported driving over a fallen cross and carrying fire on his car for nearly a block. A number of cars, unable to swerve out of the way, struck the flaming arms and sent sparks flying.

The cross found nearest to downtown was at State and Union, where it burned merrily astride a fire hydrant that was painted to look like a little policeman. Altogether, it was estimated there were almost 50 of the flaming little nui-sances.

While all this was going on, a large touring car ap-peared suddenly out of nowhere and started moving down Front Street. It carried four men wearing white hooded robes but not masks. The car also bore a number of hissing red railroad flares; they colored the night air and were reflected in the storefront windows and they cast a lurid light on the faces of the men in the car and the people in the street.

Across the back of the car, projecting about a foot on either side, was a lighted sign emblazoned with the letters KKK. The car moved slowly down the street, almost apparition-like, and the spectators were so astonished they didn't even think to take down the license plate number—if, indeed, there was one.

It halted briefly in a small traffic jam at the corner of Park Street, and a few men pressed forward to peer inside, but none could recognize the driver or his passengers, who stared stonily straight ahead, like soldiers on dress parade. Then the car speeded up and was gone, swallowed up by the night. Meanwhile, the Ku Klux Klan newspaper, "The Fiery Cross," was distributed along downtown Front Street.

Next morning, after all the furor had died down, Police Chief John Blacken and his men went looking for a man named Basil B. Carleton. Carleton was a Kleagle in the Ku Klux Klan; a paunchy potato-faced man with hair like the bristles in a carpet sweeper. He had come to town from Indiana a few months before, making no secret of the fact that he planned to recruit new members for the Klan.

From rented offices in a building on Front Street he conducted his operations—until the owners finally forced him out. Then he went underground, more or less, while still holding secret meetings and distributing Klan literature around town. There was no law against that, and the authorities were powerless to do anything about it.

Chief Blacken and his men couldn't find Carleton. He had skipped town early that morning. So City Prosecutor James J. Tweedle obtained a warrant for his arrest and sent it down to Indiana, hoping to have him extradited and put on trial in Traverse City. The charge was "possession of explosives with intent to destroy property and lives"—a felony.

Basil Carleton was a member of the so-called "new" Ku Klux Klan. It was founded by a fundamental preacher in Atlanta, Ga, in 1915. Unlike the post-Civil War Klan, which confined its activities mostly to the South, the "new" organization was influential in the North as well, especially in Indiana, Oregon and Maine.

Like the Nazis and other right-wing radical groups, the "new" Klan was anti-black, anti-Catholic, anti-Jew. They were also anti-union, anti-liberal, anti-immigrant—in short, anti everybody except native WASPs: white Anglo-Saxon Protestants.

Actually, they were closer ideologically to the "Know Nothings" of 1850-1860 than to the "old" Klan. They were mostly illiterate louts whose racial hatreds and extreme chauvinism served to demonstrate the truth of Dr. Samuel Johnson's observation that patriotism is the last refuge of a scoundrel.

Carleton was arrested in Richmond, Ind., on August 25, and two Traverse City officers went down there to get him. He went on trial on December 10, before Judge Parm Gilbert at the County Courthouse. James Tweedle handled the prosecution; local attorney Elmer B. White, assisted by a downtown lawyer, appeared for the defense.

Edwin H. Campbell, manager of the hardware department at the Hannah Lay store, testified that Basil Carleton telephoned him on the afternoon of August 7 and ordered 25 pounds of dynamite, which he had to have picked up at a warehouse outside of town. And A. E. Whitsell, an employee in that department, testified that he sold Carleton the explosive at 6:30 that evening. He said Carleton also bought some fuses and three blasting caps.

Two Traverse City men testified that they saw Carleton coming from the direction of the explosions shortly after they took place. Bob Rokos and Carl Blind were standing in front of Jud Cameron's Barbershop and Pool Hall when they saw Carleton coming down the street toward them. They said Carleton ducked into Cameron's and went out the back door to the alley. They said he was wearing a light summer suit and that the trouser bottoms were covered with burrs.

Three other local men, admittedly members of the Klan, testified that Carleton was nowhere near the scene of the explosions that evening.

After two days of testimony, the jury found Carleton not guilty; the prosecution had failed to prove its case.

Carleton was re-arrested immediately and charged with a lesser offense—setting off an explosion within the city limits without permission of the mayor: a misdemeanor. The trial took place in the offices of Justice of Peace W. W. Smith above the Chamber of Commerce before a six-man jury: Sam Iles, Jud Cameron, William Goode, Thomas Shane, Frank Trude and Harry Hibbard.

The jury failed to agree, the case was dismissed and Basil B. Carleton went back home to Indiana.

He'd had enough of Traverse City to last him a lifetime.

Traverse City had had enough of him, too, and the Ku Klux Klan as well. As far as the Klan was concerned, local people had made their sentiments clear beyond the shadow of a doubt, and the Ku Klux Klan never raised its ugly head in Traverse City again.

THE LEGENDARY
JIM HENDRYX

I remember the first time I laid eyes on him.

He was striding down Front Street in Traverse City, presumably headed for a card game at Jud Cameron's poolroom and barbershop: a tall, lean, outdoorsy man with a white handlebar mustache and keen blue eyes set in a weather beaten face — dressed in woodman's boots, ducksback breeches, a red-checked flannel shirt and Stetson hat.

I didn't know who he was, but I knew he was *somebody*.

Jim Hendryx was the stuff of dust-jacket writers' dreams. His life read better than many of the plots of his Wild West and Yukon Gold Rush novels.

Before he was out of his 20s he had sold hardware and life insurance, bought bark for a tannery, run levels on a proposed electric railway in Ohio, kept books for a sheep-shearing plant, punched cattle on several big spreads in Montana and Saskatchewan, panned gold and gambled at poker in the Yukon.

His longest continuous job was at the tannery in Kentucky. "I stayed there 53 weeks," Jim wrote, "and to this day that remains my record for holding a steady job."

Born James Beardsley Hendryx at Sauk Centre, Minnesota, in 1880—the son of Charles F. Hendryx, who was owner and publisher of the Sauk Centre Herald—Jim grew up with the town's most famous son, Sinclair Lewis.

Though perhaps not in Lewis' class as a writer, Jim as a boy and man was everything Lewis was not.

Lewis, in a boyhood diary, describes Jim this way:

"I went with Jim Hendryx on his Rural Free (mail) delivery route this morning, Jim was dressed like a 'pony express rider'—broad sombrero, brown flannel shirt open at neck & arms & belt. His face and hands are bronzed from exposure (Jim will take law at the U. of Minn. next year). He has always been a great hunter, fisher & trapper. He hunted birds eggs, fished, hunted, trapped, rode boxcars with Claude . . ."

Jim was the close friend and chief lieutenant of Claude Lewis, Sinclair's older brother, who became a famous surgeon. "Sinclair was three years younger," Jim said, "and he was a pest when we were kids. He was always wanting to drag along with us when we went anywhere. You couldn't get rid of him."

Homely, lonely, misfit Sinclair Lewis remembered it like this:

"When I was 10 or so, Claude's gang, composed of old, seasoned scouts of 15, were masters of the woods, the lake and the swimming hole in Hoboken Crick. When I tried to swim there, getting no further than bubbling and chok-

*ing, Claude's more meticulous vandals tied my clothing in
knots and painstakingly soaked it. When I climbed out of the
mud and found my knotted costume, I rose to precocious
eloquence which received from Jim Hendryx my only com-
pliment: "Gee, Harry musta swallowed the dictionary!"
(Lewis full name was Harry Sinclair Lewis.)*

After a year at the University of Minnesota (he helped
pay his expenses by running a weekend poker game, at which
even some members of the faculty were regular participants),
Jim decided the law wasn't his bag and started out on his
travels. His comment on schooling is characteristic:

"Attended public school for a vast number of years
during which I learned to fish, hunt and trap . . . then entered the University of Minnesota, where I absorbed so much
of the curriculum that even yet fragments of it work to the
surface and have to be carefully removed."

In the same autobiography sketch, his account of his
surveying experience is worth quoting verbatim:

"When I got back from Kentucky and West Virginia
without anything to do I ran into a fellow who wanted somebody to run levels on an interurban track they were putting
through. I asked him for a job.

" 'Can you run a level?' he asked.

" 'Sure,' I said, and got the job. Of course I didn't
have the slightest idea of how to run a level, so I skipped
over to the courthouse and asked a fellow I knew: 'How in
the devil do you run levels? Can I learn it?'

"He said I could in six months or so."

" 'Six months!' I said. 'I've got to learn it in two
days.'

"So he sent me over to a job and two engineers there
showed me the difference between a level and a transit. There
is a difference, as I remember, but I don't recollect what it
is."

"Well, that was on a Friday and during the next two
days I completed my engineering course and went to work

on Monday. I got along all right until I learned that in each town you had to tie in from the last station to the Government bench, which you'd always find somewhere about the courthouse. I'd never heard of it before, but my rodman was a third-year engineering student, so I told him to do it; said it'll be good experience for him. He was tickled to death and took care of it in every town. I don't know yet how you do it."

"I stayed on that job for four months and didn't do any harm, as the company went broke and couldn't pay us— so we quit."

From there Jim wandered west and got a job punching cattle on a ranch near Chinook, Montana. While riding the range, he became friendly with two notorious outlaws, Kid Curry and his brother, Lonny, and kept them supplied with coffee and tobacco in their mountain hideout.

The Curry brothers were members of the Wild Bunch, the train-robbing gang of Butch Cassidy and the Sundance Kid. A posse was formed to go after them and Jim was asked to join. He got out of it by damaging his saddle.

"There was an unwritten law that you couldn't be forced into a posse without your own saddle," Jim said. "The Currys were neighbors and I didn't want any trouble with them."

In 1898 Jim and a cowpuncher friend took off for the gold fields of Alaska and the Yukon, with a stake of $1,400 they'd won playing poker. They spent the next 14 months in the Yukon country. Jim said, "chopping cordwood, gouging gravel, playing poker and chopping cordwood.

"We didn't make much," he explained. "Got there too late and our claims were poor. And living was too high. In Dawson, in '98, eggs went to $2 apiece and flour to $100 a sack."

After making his way to Vancouver on a salmon boat and another year of punching cattle, he drifted to Cincinnati where his father was editing a newspaper, the Cincinnati

American. Jim got a job with the *Enquirer* writing feature stories, then sold his first piece of fiction and "quit punching time clocks forever."

His parting with the newspaper is a classic story. Assigned to cover the hanging of a criminal named Jenkins at Joliet, Illinois, Jim witnessed the execution and wrote the story. But he was disappointed with the headline they gave it, so he wrote his own and slipped it past a sleepy copy editor as the paper was being put to bed.

Next day Jim's headline, in all its alliterative glory, blared: "JENKINS JERKED TO JESUS AT JOLIET." Jim was quietly asked to leave.

Soon afterward, Jim married Hermione Flagler, a gifted pianist and music teacher in Cincinnati. In 1921 he bought 300 acres of forest land on Grand Traverse Bay a few miles north of Traverse City and the couple settled down in a big, rambling house that had once been a resort hotel.

There was a mile or more of Lake Michigan shoreline and, at that time, no neighbors within rifle range. Jim had fallen in love with the Northern Michigan country while on a fishing trip with Harold Titus, another Traverse City writer.

Here they started their family of two girls and a boy— Hermione, Betty and James B. Jr. Here, too, Jim embarked on an astonishing prolific writing career that produced in the next 30 years more than 70 novels and innumerable short stories of outdoor adventure.

His tales of Connie Morgan, Black John Smith, and Corporal Downey of the Royal Canadian Mounted—many of them serialized in "The American Boy"—brought delight to at least two generations of American boys (and girls). The locale of many of his stories was Halfaday Creek, so named because the sourdoughs panned gold half a day and played poker the other half.

Claude Lewis once asked Jim what was the difference between his writing and Sinclair's.

"The difference," Jim said, "is that Red gets a dollar a word, and I get a penny a word."

Nevertheless, in the 1920s he was earning from $40,000 to $50,000 a year from his writing—a very considerable sum in those days.

Many years ago on the "Information Please" program, Clifton Fadiman asked the panel, "What author is noted for hunting and fishing six months of every year?"

Sinclair Lewis raised his hand and said, "James B. Hendryx."

"That's not what I have here," said Fadiman. "My script calls for Ernest Hemingway."

"That's right," Lewis conceded. "Jim Hendryx hunts and fishes twelve months of every year."

For Jim, writing was merely a means to an end. It provided him with the money and leisure to devote much of his time to his two great loves, hunting and fishing.

Nevertheless, he was serious about his work and a careful craftsman. He made at least one trip a year to consult with top authorities of the Royal Mounted at Ottawa and to get new maps of the wilderness areas.

"I go to great pains and trouble to locate every piece of action correctly," he wrote. But I never yet wrote a story of Canada without getting a letter from some constable up on Hudson's Bay or Great Slave Lake saying, 'I liked your story but where the villain sets fire to the tepee and the beautiful Indian girl in the second chapter, the Mackenzie River runs northeast instead of northwest.' Those fellows are hell for the geography."

Stories about Jim in Traverse City—and up in Canada where the family spent their summers on remote Basswood Lake north of Thessalon—are legion. Some are unprintable, some probably apocryphal. One or two will suffice to illustrate Jim's wild, irreverent sense of fun and humor.

In the early days the Hendryx house on Lee's Point was a mile or more from any plowed road, and in winter they often had to use a horse-and-cutter or sleigh to get to town. But sometimes, when conditions were right, Jim would drive his Model T on the ice to Traverse City, 12 miles away.

He did this one year that was getting on toward spring; loaded up the car with a month's supply of groceries and headed for home on the bay ice. On the way back the car broke through the ice in 20 feet of water. Jim managed to get most of the food supplies to shore before the car sank out of sight.

A farmer came along just then and yelled, "What in the world are you doing, Jim?"

"I'm starting a grocery store, you darn fool," Jim told him. "What'd you think I was doing?"

Jim was an incurable practical joker, but nobody ever took offense because he was such fun to be with. And no one laughed louder when the joke was on him.

Jim often spent his mornings at home pecking out a story on a portable typewriter held on a piece of hardboard in his lap. Afternoons, he sometimes went into town for a card game with the boys at Jud Cameron's.

At least two or three times—according to one of his former hired men—he'd be so wrapped up in a story that he'd absent-mindedly jump in his car and back out of the garage without opening the doors. The splintering crash brought the kids running from the house and Hermione to the window, while Jim would be sitting there in the car, laughing at himself.

About himself he wrote, "For recreation I like good wine, some women—but no song—and never allow work to interfere with hunting and fishing."

He also loved kids, horses, dogs, poker and cribbage, good bourbon whiskey, and his family—not necessarily in that order. He hit the bottle pretty hard in his younger days— went on a three-day binge once with Jack London—but he swore off one day and never took another drink the rest of his life.

He was a master fly fisherman and a superb wing shot. One old friend remembers Jim as the only man he ever knew who could cast a fly around the bend in the river.

Jim was known for his colorful language. In his late years he was lured to Hollywood as the star of Ralph Edward's "This Is Your Life." The TV staff had been worried about Jim's language, and when Edwards intercepted him on Vine Street in front of the El Capitan theater, and announced that Jim was on exhibition, one of the crew was able to slip his hand in front of Jim's mustache and muffle the inevitable cuss word.

At a family gathering in the big house on Lee's Point, one of Jim's little nieces announced at the dinner table:

"I think Uncle Jim is just like God. But I guess God probably doesn't swear as much."

Jim has long ago gone to the Happy Hunting Ground, and I hope he has found everything he wanted there, including plenty of canvasback ducks and speckled trout. One of Jim's lifelong friends summed him up best:

"Jim Hendryx was born 100 years too late but made the best of it. He was at heart a mountain man, a fur trader, an outlaw of the plains. He was everlastingly a boy—not a Boy Scout, more a Huckleberry Finn."

That was Jim—one of the best.

AL CAPONE
SLEPT HERE

Even gangsters, it seems, have to take vacations. Scarface Al Capone, infamous king of the Chicago underworld back in the twisted '20s, had a half dozen hideouts in northern Michigan and Wisconsin where he could relax and get away from it all.

One of Capone's favorite retreats was a densely wooded 10 acres along Lake Michigan about two miles south of the harbor town of Leland in northwest Lower Michigan. The old Capone hideout consists mainly of two large two-story cottages about 50 yards apart in a clearing on the bluff above Lake Michigan beach. Between the cottages and the main road, M-22, lies a quarter mile of thick, second-growth maple and beech. A two-track country lane leads through it to a rusty gate some 400 feet east of the cottage.

When Capone and his gang were "in residence," an armed sentry manned the gate day and night and there was a private telephone line to the cottages; all visitors were carefully screened.

Other security measures included a 30-foot observation tower. It still stands on a steep conical hill just north and east of the clearing, guarding all approaches by land and water. A well-worn path leads up to it through the woods. In Capone's day, old-timers say, a heavy machinegun was mounted on the topmost landing.

Guarding the approaches a little farther north and east is a small body of water, Duck Lake. The impregnability of the place is impressive. When it came to security, Capone seems to have thought of everything.

Over the years a body of legend has grown up about the place, and it's difficult to separate fact from fiction. It is certain, however, that Capone and his men stayed there several summers in the late '20s and early '30s. Several local people remember seeing him.

Many of the old summer cottages along the lake here were given sentimental names by their owners. In the old days, the Capone hideaway was known as "Heartsease." Some people still call it by that name.

Was there, after all, a streak of tenderness in this man Capone; could the same man who could beat to death with a baseball bat three henchmen who had plotted against him name a cottage "Heartsease?"

Not really. Capone had nothing to do with naming the place. That was the work of little Rosalind English, 12, who scratched "Heartsease by the Lake" with a sharp stick or a nail in fresh concrete at the doorstep of one of the cottages in 1915.

Rosalind was the only child of one of Indiana's first families. Her father, William E. English, owned the English Hotel and Opera House on Monument Circle in downtown Indianapolis. Captain Billy English was a state senator and a prominent Indianapolis businessman.

He got his military title from service in the Spanish-American War, from which he returned a hero in 1898 after being almost fatally injured near Santiago, Cuba. The horse he was riding was shot from under him, pinning him beneath it. It was said that the same piece of shrapnel also wounded his good friend, Teddy Roosevelt.

In addition to his Indianapolis holdings, English owned the family's ancestral home, Englishton Park, an 800-acre estate in Southern Indiana. He was a millionaire several times over. His father, William H. English, also a leader in Indiana politics, had been a Democrat candidate for vice-president in 1880 and was a writer of ability.

How did this illustrious, blue-blooded Hoosier family get mixed up with Al Capone?

In 1898, Capt. English had married Helen Orr, a beautiful, but rather unstable woman of 24; he was 47. A month later he went off to war. They were divorced soon after he returned, but remarried a few months later.

Their married life seems to have been stormy. Divorced again in 1910, they remarried again in 1924. Their only child, Rosalind, was born in 1903.

Capt. English built Heartsease in 1915. From then until 1924 the English family spent most of their summers there, dividing the rest of their time between their suite in the English Hotel and the 23-room mansion in Englishton Park. At Heartsease, English lived in one cottage, Rosalind and her mother in the other.

Rosalind's death in an auto accident in 1924 was a terrible blow to her parents (she'd been responsible for getting them back together in 1923). English himself died two years later.

Under terms of his will, the income from his estate went to his wife during her lifetime. After her death the entire estate was to go to a charitable foundation to be used to erect a building housing all organized charities in Indianapolis (the English Foundation Building), and also to maintain at Englishton Park a home for "poor and indigent girls."

April 10, 1928, Mrs. English, 56, married Frank J. Prince, 40, an *Indianapolis Times* reporter who had won a $1,000 prize she offered for "outstanding investigative work by an Indiana reporter." In a series of articles, Prince exposed corruption among high Indiana officials bribed by the Ku Klux Klan. Mrs. English described the marriage as the "culmination of a beautiful romance."

However, she divorced Prince four months later, charging cruelty and incompatibility. Then, repeating the pattern of her first marriage, she remarried him the following year.

Prince, a suave, charming, articulate man, wasn't what he seemed. Between 1908 and 1925 he had served five prison terms — for theft, embezzlement, issuing bogus checks and parole violations — in the Indiana Reformatory and Joliet prison. A native of New York, he had moved to Chicago in his youth. Many of his crimes were committed there, where he had connection with the Capone mob. His real name was Morris Czech, and he had used many other aliases besides Prince.

In February, 1932, Mrs. Helen English Prince made out a new will, leaving everything to "my beloved husband, Frank J. Prince." She died four months later in Los Angeles, where the couple had stopped enroute to a vacation in Hawaii.

Early in the morning she was stricken in their hotel room and taken to the hospital; she never regained consciousness. Ill the week before, she was seemingly on the road to recovery when she suffered the collapse. The coroner who performed the autopsy said the cause of death was "probably an accidental overdose of sleeping pills;" she was known to have been using the drug.

Prince inherited his wife's personal fortune, which included Heartsease. In 1934 he sued to gain the entire English estate as well, but the claim was denied.

After a year or two of heading a detective agency in Chicago and an advertising agency in New York, specializing in bookmatch promotions, he acquired with borrowed money the Universal Match Company, a multi-million-dollar firm in St. Louis.

Over the years, subsidiary corporations were added to form one of the earliest "conglomerates." By the middle '50s, Prince had become well known as a wealthy New York industrialist and served as a "dollar-a-year" man in President Dwight D. Eisenhower's administration.

His criminal record came back to haunt him, however, in 1960, when he gave $500,000 to Washington University in St. Louis for a building to be named in his honor. Ted Link, a tough, ex-Marine crime reporter for the *St. Louis Post-Dispatch,* dug into Prince's past and broke the story. Prince admitted his prison record, but said that his life had been blameless since then. His distress over the expose' brought him much sympathy in the press.

"This is vicious," said Richard Amberg, publisher of the *St. Louis Globe-Democrat.* "The dirtiest piece of Godd--- journalism I've ever seen." *Time* magazine quoted Amberg and also called it a low blow.

His later life may have been exemplary, but he was the link between the patrician English family of Indianapolis and Al Capone. It was with Prince's OK that Capone used Heartsease as a summer hideaway between 1928 and 1932.

MISSING

What Happened to Ralph Anderson?

His family was waiting for him at the Pere Marquette depot, but when the train pulled in, Ralph Anderson wasn't on it. Orpha Anderson and their two small children were disappointed, but not greatly alarmed. Before he left for Chicago, Anderson had told his wife to expect him on Wednesday evening, but not to be alarmed if he was delayed a day or two.

And, indeed, when they got home that evening, they found a letter from him in the mail saying that he didn't see how he could make it home before Thursday night. He said he might stop at Constantine, Mich., on the way back to buy some caskets for his mortuary business.

But that evening Mrs. Anderson got a telephone call from Captain Mackay of the S. S. *Alabama*. He told her that her husband had registered aboard on Tuesday evening for the trip from Chicago to Muskegon, but that he was not on board when the ship docked at Muskegon. Mackay suggested the possibility of suicide.

"Nonsense!" Mrs. Anderson told him. Suicide was unthinkable. What must have happened, she said, was that her husband had probably checked in early for the voyage, then gone ashore to attend to some last minute business, and missed the boat.

That was a possibility, Captain Mackay conceded.

Anderson was a member of one of Traverse City's pioneer families. His grandfather, Samuel Anderson, had brought his family here from New York in 1866 and set himself up in the wagon and carriage making business. Ralph's father, William S. Anderson, operated a mortuary in 1883 under the name of W. S. Anderson & Son. Ralph took over the business when his father retired in 1896.

Now, at age 38, he was one of Traverse City's most successful businessmen.

He had left Traverse City on the train on a business trip to Chicago, on Sunday, June 8, 1919. Among other things, he planned to buy some building material. Just a few weeks previously he had purchased the Columbia Transfer Company, a local freight and passenger service, and planned to build a large new garage for his vehicles. He took the train to Muskegon, then embarked on the *Alabama* for Chicago, arriving there early Monday morning.

On Thursday evening, having heard nothing from her husband, Mrs. Anderson was frantic with worry. She telephoned her brother-in-law, Frank Emlaw in Muskegon, thinking her husband might have stopped there, but Emlaw had neither seen nor heard from him. She also called the casket factory in Constantine; they hadn't seen him either. Meanwhile, the authorities in Chicago had been notified, and were conducting an investigation there. Close friends of the family, Milton D. Bryant, president of Ford agency, and Lewis Stocking, superintendent of the Metropolitan Life Insurance agency left for Chicago on Friday morning to find out what they could.

Interviewed by reporters, Mrs. Anderson said that it was preposterous to think that her husband would take his own life. His letter from Chicago seemed to have been written in a very happy mood. He said he had lunched that day (Monday) with Traverse City people, Mrs. James T. Milliken and Dr. Thomas. He reported that the business trip was satisfactory and he expected to be home soon. He admonished Bobby to be a good boy.

His wife told reporters that he had no financial troubles, that he was in excellent health, that he had everything in the world to live for. "Certainly something must have happened to him," she cried. "He had a matter in court this week that needed his personal attention, and nothing short of an accident could have kept him away."

She said that he had a diamond ring worth $350 on his finger, and probably a considerable amount of cash. Her fear, she said, was that he had met with foul play.

Meanwhile, the steamship company reported that his luggage had been found intact in his stateroom; and it was known now that the only things missing were a dark summer suit and a pair of shoes.

In Chicago, Bryant and Stocking hired the Pinkertons to make a thorough investigation.

After several days, the detective agency reported that they had traced Anderson's movement up to the time he registered on the *Alabama;* the trail ended there. No one could be found who had actually seen him on board. The boat left Chicago Tuesday evening, June 10th at 7:45. It docked at Grand Haven from 3:30 to 5 a.m., then arrived at Muskegon two hours later.

The search was finally abandoned on the first of July.

Ralph Anderson was never seen or heard from again. One of the more plausible theories about his disappearance was that he was knocked unconscious, robbed, and thrown overboard by some thug. But there is no evidence to support it.

The story has a bizarre epilogue.

Two years later, a traveling magician and self-avowed clairvoyant, one Professor Khayam, announced that he had information on the whereabouts of Ralph Anderson. He said that he would reveal the secret during the performance of his Saturday night show in Traverse City. To a packed theatre that night he revealed that Ralph Anderson, under the assumed name of Carl Lundstrom, was alive and well and living a new life in San Francisco. More information could be obtained by writing Robert E. Kane, 605 Pantages Bldg., San Francisco. He also stated that Anderson was employed at 752 Market St. in that city.

Although he placed little credence in the Professor's tale, Judge Fred Pratt, in whose court Anderson's estate was under probate felt obliged to check it out. He wrote a friend, Dr. V. C. Thomas, who had moved from Traverse City to San Francisco and was now practicing medicine there.

Two weeks later, Judge Pratt had his answer. The Pantages Bldg. address of Robert E. Kane, Thomas wrote, was actually the address of "Billboard," the entertainment-world magazine. The editor of that magazine had recently received word that all messages for Robert E. Kane (whom the editor had never heard of) should be forwarded to G. H. Bryant of East Jordan, Mich.

The doctor also wrote that the address where Anderson (or Lundstrom) was employed belonged to a firm called the Moss Glove House. Needless to say, they had never heard of Lundstrom either.

It was obvious, wrote the doctor, that Professor Khayam, Robert Kane, and G. H. Bryant were one and the same person —and that the magician was the perpetrator of a cruel hoax.

In the absence of conclusive proof that her husband was dead, Mrs. Anderson was years in recovering her husband's life insurance. She finally had to take the Illinois life insurance firm to court in that state, and eventually obtained a judgment in her favor.

A Child Is Missing

When 6-year-old Douglas Holmes disappeared one midsummer afternoon, the people of Elk Rapids thought first that he had drowned in the river, then that he had been kidnapped by gypsies.

One Friday afternoon, July 8, 1927, Douglas and his mother were fishing below the powerhouse dam in the river on the north side of town. Around four o'clock Douglas said he was tired of fishing and left to go see his father, Harry J. Holmes, who owned a garage and Chevrolet agency downtown.

His mother last saw him crossing a nearby bridge. A little later, a friend of the family, elderly Joe Tudcott, saw him sitting on the front steps of Winter's drugstore, chewing on a stick of licorice. After that he dropped out of sight.

At five o'clock the mother gathered up the fishing gear and went home to cook supper. Her husband arrived half an hour later but said he'd seen nothing of Douglas. He sat down to supper but his wife began to worry and went out to look for her son. It wasn't like him to be late for meals.

She spent the next half hour walking the streets and questioning everyone she met. Then, frantic with worry, she notified the authorities. The authorities consisted solely of Deputy Sheriff A. G. Maxwell. Under his direction the whole town turned out to look for the missing child. On the assumption that Douglas was somewhere in the river, teams of men in small boats dragged the length of it, poking into every nook and cranny along the banks and probing the deep holes with long poles. Others searched the woods nearby. The search continued by flashlight long after dark.

Next day, a woman who lived on a farm seven miles north of town reported that she had seen a large touring car speeding past her place around five o'clock the previous afternoon. A woman was driving, she said, and the man beside her was holding a small boy between his knees. The child was screaming and kicking and waving his arms.

She said she distinctly heard the man say, "Shut up! We're not going to hurt you." The man was wearing a dark suit and a dark felt hat. Both had swarthy complexions. The rear seat was piled with luggage and camping gear.

Two farm neighbors confirmed her story, saying they too had seen the car and heard the child's cries.

Later, a Traverse City man, Clyde McIntyre, reported seeing a black Hudson touring car parked in front of Hotel Traverse on Friday noon. A dark-skinned woman was seated behind the wheel, wearing a strange looking scarf over her head. A man of similar appearance, apparently her husband, came from across the street and got in beside her.

"A couple of gypsies," McIntyre said to himself., and thought no more about it until he read the newspaper story next day.

Then somebody remembered that the town had trouble with a band of gypsies the previous year. They were escorted out of town, and as they left, one sinister-looking fellow shouted, "We'll come back and get this town and get it good!"

Was this a case of gypsy vengeance?

Meanwhile, a professional diver had searched the river bottom, and the deep holes were blasted with dynamite without revealing a trace of the missing boy. A tip from a clairvoyant in Cadillac, that the body was caught in the river under some tree roots near the small bridge leading to the island, likewise came to nothing.

The authorities were sure now that Douglas had been kidnapped. "It's beyond the shadow of a doubt," said Harvey Walcott, a FBI agent in Traverse, who had joined the investigation. A nationwide alert with the boy's description was sent out, and the story made headlines all over the country.

A reward of $100 was posted by the boy's distraught parents. This was later increased to $500 by public donation fund set up by the bank.

The police, now augmented by a State Trooper, ran down numerous leads that led nowhere. They investigated a band of gypsies camped near Cadillac and another group of campers (who turned out not to be gypsies) near Lake City. The boy's grandfather, A. B. Fairbanks, was sent to Mackinaw City with a photograph of Douglas, but nobody there—including the carferry personnel—could recall seeing either the boy or the car.

On Friday, a week after the boy's disappearance, the police had to admit they were stumped. Every avenue of inquiry had led down a blind alley. Nevertheless, though it now seemed hopeless of finding the boy alive, the search would continue.

It came to an end two days later. A man walking on the beach three miles north of Elk Rapids noticed a flock of crows wheeling and cawing over something up the shore. Ed Anderson, a 50-year-old Indian, knew what that meant. He investigated and found the body of a small boy on the sand. Nearby was a beached raft. He ran all the way to town to summon the sheriff and the coroner.

As they pieced the story together later, Douglas, who could not swim, must have been swept out on the raft to deeper water by a sudden gust of wind. Afterward, several small boys admitted to having seen him playing on the raft; and a 12-year-old girl told her father she had seen him on the raft the day he disappeared. Somehow the report never reached the authorities.

How long he had survived his ordeal on the raft was impossible to tell. The coroner's finding was death by drowning.

The people of Elk Rapids shared the parents' grief. They knew that one of the hardest things for parents to bear is the loss of a child. And the really awful thing about this particular loss, they said, was that at a time when the search for him was at its most intense, the boy was out on the bay on a raft, no doubt yelling his lungs out for help—and that if they had only known it, or guessed it, he might easily have been saved.

But that was something no one wanted to think about.

Ed Anderson collected the reward. But instead of $500 he got only $100. Bank president C. B. Carver explained that the contributions had been made with the condition that most of the money would be returned if Douglas was found drowned, not kidnapped.

Pete Rennie Vanishes

When prominent Traverse City businessman and sportsman Ferris J. "Pete" Rennie disappeared one April day in 1965, most people assumed he had fallen through the ice on Grand Traverse Bay and drowned. But there were some who insisted his disappearance was voluntary, and that he'd gone off to start a new life.

At the time of his disappearance Rennie was general manager of the Rennie Oil Company, a firm founded by his father, Charles Rennie. The Rennies were one of the area's oldest families. Pete's grandfather, John "Black Jack" Rennie, long time city police chief, was one of the most colorful characters in Traverse City history.

At 48, Pete was in the prime of life — attractive, well educated, articulate and athletic, a lover of the outdoors whose favorite pastime was yachting. In 1959, the Rennie Oil Co. purchased Marion Island in Grand Traverse Bay from another local firm, Parts Manufacturing Co., which had logged off the island's virgin timber during World War II. The purchase was made largely through Pete's initiative, and the island became one of his favorite projects.

Under his supervision the island was developed as a wilderness park, with picnic and camping facilities, a boat dock, nature trails and wildlife refuge, all open to the public. It was hoped that preservation of the remaining timber would continue to provide a sanctuary for the great bald eagles that had made the island their home for generations.

To help with this work Rennie hired Ralph Matthews, a former Texas oil rigger and sailor. Matthews and his tiny Indian wife Clara were installed in a rustic island house as caretakers. (Matthews' lifelong dream of sailing around the world had been cruelly shattered when, a year or two previously, his hand-built 35-foot sloop Manda was crushed in the ice while moored for the winter at the Rennie Oil dock.)

Rennie was a frequent visitor to the island both winter and summer. He made regular trips to discuss development plans with Matthews, bring him supplies, and take him and his wife to Traverse City from time to time. When the Bay was frozen, he travelled on an airplane-propeller-driven amphibious sled. He was in daily communication with Matthews between the oil company terminal and the island by means of a two-way radio.

Rennie spent Sunday night, April 12, 1965, on the island visiting with the Matthewses. It wasn't until the wee hours of the morning that he left the island to return home.

Later, Matthews said: "It must have been around two in the morning when Pete decided to go home. He said goodbye and kissed my wife—not on the lips, mind you; he was always a perfect gentleman—and took off. We knew the ice was bad but we didn't worry about him on that sled."

He arrived home safely and went to bed. But next morning he decided to return to the island, and his wife Marilyn was unable to persuade him not to go. He set out on the sled around 10 o'clock. She watched him from the livingroom windows of their Greilickville home on the water as the sled headed east and grew smaller and smaller in the distance. The ice was dark and rotten (it went out on April 20 that year). But Pete was safe as long as he stayed with the amphibious sled.

Half an hour later she looked out and was surprised to see the sled still on the ice. It was just a small black dot south of the island but it wasn't moving and she could see nothing of her husband. Extremely worried she called the sheriff and sounded the alarm.

A helicopter, dispatched by the Coast Guard, found the sled and hovered over it for several minutes but made no attempt to land on the rotten ice. There was no sign of Rennie.

Later that afternoon, two sheriff deputies, Jack Canfield and Ron Sanford, made their way slowly out to the sled, wearing wet suits and dragging a small aluminum boat. It took them almost four hours. They found the sled on the ice about a mile from the Old Mission peninsula shore and a mile or so south of Marion Island. Near it, running north and south, was a wide crack of open water.

They also found footprints in the soft ice. They led north along the lead of open water for about 200 yards. Here the crack narrowed to just a few feet—and the footprints came to an end. They could find no tracks on the opposite side of the open water, but there was a man's cap floating there and a life jacket. They found another life preserver in the water several yards away.

The two men returned to the sled and tried to start the engine. It turned over readily enough—and there was plenty of gas—but then it misfired and failed to run at full speed. Later, after the sled was towed ashore by a military landing craft, it was found to have faulty fuel valves.

Pete Rennie was never seen or heard from again.

But as often happens when some prominent person drops out of sight, people claim to have seen the missing party in various places. Over the next few years Pete was "seen" in such faraway places as Mexico, Alaska and Italy.

The trouble with such reports is that when you attempt to track the eye witnesses down, the trail gets very faint indeed. It's always someone's friend or friend of a friend who saw the missing person. And if you are persistent enough to track down the actual eyewitness, it turns out to be somebody who tells you, "I didn't actually speak to him, but it sure looked like him anyway."

Canfield scoffs at such reports.

"The ice was so spongy and rotten that day," he says, "that nobody in his right mind would be playing games out there. That was a very dangerous situation. It took us all that time to reach the sled because we'd fall through the ice every few feet. We must have gone down at least 50 times before we got there."

Canfield reasons that after his sled stopped running, Rennie followed the open lead on foot, looking for a place to cross. When he reached the place where it narrowed, he may have tried to jump across and fell through the ice or into the open water.

"Nobody could have lived in that water more than a few minutes," Canfield said. "And it would have been next to impossible to climb out on that rotten ice."

WILLIAM S. HART
PLAYED HERE

Anyone old enough to remember William S. Hart, remembers him as the first of the famous cowboy movie stars — remembers seeing him in the leading role of such epic horse-operas as *Wild Bill Hickock, Two-Gun Hicks, O'Malley of the Mounted* and *Tumbleweeds.* All this for ten cents apiece plus a nickel for a bag of popcorn on Saturday afternoons in the late teens and twenties. Hart was the prototype of the strong, silent man of the West. The movies were silent, too, way back then.

Yet the only horse in his background was the one he drove on the seat of an ice wagon in the streets of New York in the hot, dusty summer of 1894.

Born in Newburgh, N.Y., in 1872, Hart went to the City at the age of 19, seeking a career in the theatre. Like most would-be actors without professional experience, he had a hard time of it at first, subsisting on bit parts in season and taking any job he could find to keep body and soul together in the off-season. Besides delivering ice, he stoked the boilers in a shoe factory and posed infrequently for art classes at three dollars an hour, which was a lot of money in those days.

In the early summer of 1895, Hart noticed a small ad in one of the theatre trade papers: "Wanted—Special attraction —Steinberg's Opera House—Traverse City, Michigan."

Hart wrote later: "I neither was nor had any attraction. But I needed money badly and I thought I might as well have a crack at it. I had nothing to lose."

He wrote Julius Steinberg and was surprised to receive a prompt and encouraging reply. "I never could account for this," Hart wrote. "Unless mine was the only answer to his advertisement."

The main problem was the $16 railroad fare from New York to Traverse City. He solved it by pawning most of his winter clothing. The trip took 36 hours, and Hart said the only meal he could afford enroute was a bag of popcorn and water. "The water swelled the popcorn and filled my stomach, so I didn't suffer much." It wasn't the first time he'd gone that long without a meal. He arrived at Traverse City virtually penniless.

Realizing that he must put on a prosperous front, Hart went straight to the Park Place Hotel and engaged its finest accommodation at $10.50 a week with meals. Then he walked downtown to meet Steinberg.

Julius Steinberg had come to Traverse City in 1868 as a poor immigrant from Czarist Russia. After starting out as a pedlar with a pack on his back, selling household necessities door to door, he became one of Traverse City's most prosperous merchants. In 1894 he built the Steinberg Block, a three-story building on Front Street, with his clothing store at street level and the opera house above it for his wife, who was musically talented. It opened on December 11, 1894, with a first-rate production of *Hamlet*.

The two men hit it off right from the start. It took them less than an hour to reach a satisfactory agreement.

"He was to provide the cast from local talent," Hart said, "I to star, direct, rehearse and produce an 'attraction' to show on the Fourth of July, just three weeks from that day. We'd go 50-50 on the receipts.

"I went to work immediately, meanwhile eating every meal at the Park Place unless invited to dine somewhere else. And in those three weeks—perhaps because the local newspaper heralded me as a 'prominent New York theatrical man whom Mr. Steinberg has induced to aid him in this special at-traction—the hotel manager did not ask me for my bill."

The production was duly staged on the Fourth of July. It consisted of three parts. Hart himself opened the program with a recitation entitled "Alaska", dressed in a western costume, for which he had paid a New York costumer two dollars for a three-weeks' rental.

Hart played Romeo in the balcony scene from *Romeo and Juliet* in the second feature, and Armonde in *Camille* by Dumas in the third.

The production was an unqualified success. The receipts grossed $404 before expenses, with $151 as Hart's share. After paying his hotel bill and other expenses he returned to New York with about $100 in his pocket.

"And then," Hart said, "I owned New York. It was the most money I ever had at one time since I started acting."

Hart's performance in Traverse City was a major stepping stone to fame and fortune. In the following year he formed his own company and toured the country, gaining recognition over the years as one of the most talented young actors in America. In 1914 he went to Hollywood. Until then he and his troupe played Traverse City almost every year.

In recalling those days, Hart said, "I remember Julius Steinberg in particular. He was a kind and friendly man and the type of fellow one enjoyed speaking to. One day I was talking to him in the opera house. We were looking out the back window. There was a stream that ran behind the building. I asked him, 'Are there any fish in it?' and he said 'Oh, yes. Lots of fish.'

'What kind?' I asked him.

'Suckers,' he said.

'Oh,' I said, 'then you get them from both ends of the building.'

"The old man thought for a few moments, mumbling 'Suckers . . . both ends . . .' Then suddenly he got the point and broke out laughing. I really believe he thought it was the funniest thing he ever heard. For the next four days he insisted on telling the joke to everyone who came in the store."

Hart concluded: "My memories of Traverse City are truthfully among the most pleasant in my life, not merely because of the success I encountered there, but because I met and came to know so many nice people. They extended to me, at a most welcome time, a kindness and hospitality that I can never forget."

Hart died in 1946, and the Steinberg Opera House was destroyed by fire in 1963.

DEATH
IN THE U.P.

In early November 1898, a party of
13 Traverse City deer hunters chartered a boat to take them
to Naubinway in Michigan's Upper Peninsula. There was
nothing very unusual about that except for the boat ride—
most Traverse area hunters travelled to their deer camps in
the U.P. by railroad, crossing the straits of Mackinac on the
railroad ferry. In any case, one way or another, serious deer
hunters in all of lower Michigan went up north to do their
hunting. If you wanted a better than even chance of getting
a deer, that was the place to go.

That was because deer were very scarce even in the
northern part of lower Michigan. Seventy-five years of what

amounted to clear-cut logging had raised hob with the habitat. This, together with virtually unrestricted hunting, had almost wiped out the herd. In 1900, Michigan's deer population was estimated at a mere 50,000. Compared to 3.2 million white-tails today, that was getting dangerously close to extinction.

The boat chartered by the hunting party was the *Onekama,* a 45-foot steamer that ran a regular freight and passenger service on Grand Traverse Bay during the summer season. She was owned and operated by Capt. Joe Emory, who, after securing his vessel at the Naubinway dock, joined the hunting party for the duration of the hunting season.

They were all conveyed into the woods to the hunting camp on sleds drawn by teams of horses. The camp was an old logging shanty a few miles north of Naubinway, and they stayed there for the entire season, from November 8 to November 30. Altogether, they killed 32 deer, including at least 11 does and yearling fawns. Michigan's deer hunting license, permitting the holder to take five deer of either sex, cost 50c.

The party was late getting started on the voyage home. A big storm on the lake held them up for two or three days, and friends and relatives in Traverse City began to fear for their safety, especially after a rumor started circulating that the boat had gone down with all hands in the storm. The loss of 14 family men would have been a terrible tragedy for the community, so there was a feeling of great relief when the *Onekama* was sighted coming over the horizon on Grand Traverse Bay on December 3rd. A large crowd assembled at Hannah, Lay dock to meet her.

Some time later, a commercial photographer took a marvelous picture of the boat and its passengers. The proud hunters, rifles in hand, are standing in line on the upper deck, while just below them on the starboard side, a string of dead deer hangs almost the length of the boat. In a way that the hunters probably would never have understood, the photo is a powerful indictment of the mindless slaughter of Michigan deer in the 19th century.

Meanwhile, some three weeks earlier, another Traverse City deer hunting party, camped within a few miles of the Naubinway group, met with real tragedy. A prominent district court judge was shot dead.

Judge Roscoe L. Corbett was born in Maine in 1855 and came to Michigan with his parents in 1867. After a law degree at the University of Michigan he practiced law in Boyne City for several years, then moved to Traverse City in 1894 to be closer to the center of his judicial activities. In 1895 he gained state-wide recognition as the presiding judge in a sensational murder trial at Traverse City: State vs Woodruff Parmalee. A twice-divorced local man was tried and convicted of killing Julia Curtis, a young farm girl who was pregnant with his child.

On Wednesday, November 2, Judge Corbett and his 17-year-old son left Traverse City on the train to visit their hunting camp at Ozark, near Trout Lake Junction. They spent a day or two putting the camp in order before they were joined by other members of the party, including David Kuhns, Corbett's best friend, and Dr. A. J. DeLacy.

On the afternoon of November 7, Corbett and his son were walking with loaded guns on a logging road in the woods near the camp. A shot rang out and the judge cried out, "My God, I'm killed!" and fell to the ground. Charles ran for help from other members of the party, and together they carried his father back to camp. Dr. DeLacy examined the injured man, who remained conscious, and found that the wound was mortal—the bullet had entered Corbett's back and exited at the pit of his stomach. There was nothing anyone could do to save his life.

For two hours Kuhns sat beside the dying man's bed and tried to comfort him, while Corbett drifted in and out of consciousness. Then, about five o'clock, the judge, opening

his eyes, recognized his friend and indicated there was something he wanted to tell him. Putting his arm around Kuhn's
neck, he drew him down close to his lips.

"Goodbye, old friend," he whispered in his ear, and
died.

A short time after the accident Charles said that he
thought he had seen a hunter sitting on a stump back in the
woods, and a deer on the opposite side of the road, but he
couldn't be sure. One of the hunters made a wide circle
through the woods around the spot where Corbett fell, but
found no suspicious tracks in the snow. All were convinced
that it must have been a stray bullet, fired at some distance.

Corbett's body, in a plain pine box obtained at Trout
Lake Junction, was accompanied on the train back to Traverse
City by his grief-stricken son and other members of the party.
In order to avoid an 8-hour layover at Walton Junction, a
special train was dispatched from Traverse City to bring
them and the body home.

At first, son Charles came under the irrational suspicion that it was he who, accidentally or otherwise, fired the
fatal shot. This was complete disproved by the autopsy, which
revealed that Corbett had been shot by a rifle bullet, while
everyone knew that Charles was carrying a shotgun loaded
with buckshot. Corbett's gun, undischarged, was lying on
the ground where he fell.

Nevertheless, a small cloud of suspicion hung over
the young man's innocent head for many years—until 1915,
in fact, when a man in Alpena confessed on his deathbed
that he had accidentally fired the shot.

THE PASSENGER PIGEON
IN MICHIGAN

They came like a sudden spring storm, darkening the sky. Birds, millions and millions of birds, so many that they eclipsed the sun and filled the air with their cries, drowning out all other sound. It was the annual spring migration of the passenger pigeon from their winter quarters in the Gulf states from Texas to Florida. As far as we know, the world has never seen anything like it, before or since.

In an attempt to take some measure of their vast number, the great ornithologist John James Audubon calculated that a flock of pigeons one mile wide—which was below the average width—passing a given point at 60 miles per hour for three hours and allowing two birds per square yard, would contain about 1,250,135,000 pigeons. And that was just one flock of many.

The great spectacle was reported in the early 1600s by French explorers Cartier and Champlain. To the Pilgrims the birds were a mixed blessing. In 1643, they descended on the Plymouth crops with such voracity as to cause a serious threat of famine. Yet, five years later, when the crops failed, they saved the settlers from starvation.

In Michigan they were an important source of food for both Indians and early white settlers. The pigeon was a good-sized bird, somewhat larger than a mourning dove. The Indians preserved their flesh by drying or smoking, the whites by packing them in salt or by canning.

In 1855, North Unity, a small colony of Czech immigrants in Leelanau County on Lake Michigan south of Leland, was saved by the bell so to speak, with the late April arrival of the passenger pigeons. One of them, Joseph Krubner, wrote about it as follows:

"That first winter was very hard. Lake Michigan froze, and we were cut off from all civilization. It came a time when there wasn't any more food in our village. F. Kraitz and V. Musil and a few more men with sleds crossed the ice to the Manitou Islands, where they bought a few bushels of potatoes.

"For a while the hungry wolves were chased away from our doors. But when the potatoes were gone, hunger struck again. By the time it reached its peak, we were saved by a flock of wild pigeons. Everyone who had a gun was shooting them." Later they were able to vary their pigeon diet with fish caught in small inland lakes nearby.

A heavily wooded area near Northport was a favorite nesting and feeding ground for the birds. William Joseph Thomas wrote of the pigeons in his history of the Thomas family:

"The first twelve years we were here, from 1856 to

1868, we used to see vast numbers of wild pigeons all through the warm season of the year, from early spring till the first snow. It was a grand sight in the spring just as the snow was disappearing and the sun was bright and warm, to go out about nine o'clock in the morning and watch the pigeons flying. The first appearance would not be large. But in a few days the flight would begin at sunrise, and seen the whole sky would be alive with pigeons flying as close together as they could fly. This would keep up until noon. The next day would be the same all over again. The flights would continue for one or two weeks.

"Hundreds of thousands of pigeons would stay in our county all summer, feeding on all the nuts and berries they could find. The first few years we were here, the pigeons were only hunted and killed for home consumption, but later they had a market value and a great many people were engaged in catching them."

Payson Wolfe, a direct descendant of a long list of great Ottawa chiefs, was the champion pigeon hunter and shooter of the northland. His home stood on a hill overlooking Grand Traverse Bay near Northport. At dawn's early light, as the wild pigeons came skimming over the treetops, Payson was there to meet them.

"Armed with his famous muzzle-loading, double-barrel shotgun and always accompanied by a number of his dozen children, he took his stand at the edge of the cliff-like hill," his daughter Etta wrote. "The children carried two big clothes baskets in which to gather the game. We frequently gathered upwards of 70 birds at one discharge of his gun, but I have heard my mother say that once she saw him down 124 birds at one shot, and she was a truthful woman."

She said that her father killed birds faster than the rest of the family could take care of them, and soon their yard would be filled with mounds of pigeons. Mrs. Wolfe and some of the older children would sort and dress the birds. Payson never went to breakfast until he had bagged from 1,000 to 1,200 pigeons.

"In the small town of Northport numbering about 200 persons, practically every one got some birds, but my father was the only one who brought them down by the hundred," she said.

As railroad transportation to northern Michigan improved after 1870, professional hunters—so called "pigeoners"—came from every part of the country. Among them was a man named Wrisley, from Connecticut, who made so much money catching the birds and shipping them live to trap-shooters clubs that he was able to retire on the profits. He took up residence in Northport and lived comfortably there for the rest of his life. Some of his descendants still live there.

All this activity, however, made hardly a dent in the wild pigeon population. It wasn't until the arrival of the market hunters that the real slaughter began. With so much product available for the taking, it was inevitable that American entrepreneurs would figure out a way to capitalize on it. From a sport providing food for the family table, pigeon hunting soon became an industry employing thousands of people.

For the market hunter, guns were slow and inefficient. He used trap nets. Feeding, roosting, and nesting areas were readily identified, and the market hunters would invade the area, making feeding beds which would attract the birds in great numbers.

The bed, usually about 12 to 16 feet wide and 20 to 24 feet long, varied with the size of the net. It was carefully cleared of grass, weeds and underbrush, and baited with corn. Close by, but usually 50 feet from the bed, a blind or brush house was built. One end of the net was staked down, while the other was tied to spring poles planted in the ground. A line tied to the leading edge of the net ran to a "catch" stake at the brush house. When enough birds had gathered on the bed, the "catch" was tripped and spring poles threw the net over the feeding birds.

An essential part of the pigeoners' trade tools was the

stool pigeon. This was a live bird tethered to a box or other support in the middle of the bed. By an ingenious arrangement of cords and pulleys it could be made to flap its wings and to rise three feet from the ground. Its sole purpose was to attract other birds to the feeding bed.

At one nesting site in Grand Traverse County in 1875, some 900 people were employed trapping live birds, and killing and shipping "squabs" (young pigeons) for big city markets. That same year, from nesting sites in Newaygo, Oceana and Grand Traverse counties, 1,000 tons or 2 million squabs were shipped to market. Another 2,400,000 birds were trapped and shipped live all over the country.

Something had to give. As the flocks grew smaller and smaller with the passing years, people wondered what was happening. One theorist proclaimed that the birds had migrated to Australia. The last of the big flights in the Northport area took place in 1877, and in the following year at Petoskey. At that time there were about 5,000 commercial pigeoners pursuing the fabulous birds every year. Of that number, it is estimated that between 400 and 500 showed up at Petoskey for what turned out to be the last big kill. A few small scattered flocks continued to appear, but their numbers grew smaller every year.

Who killed the passenger pigeon? What drove the species into extinction? The answer is still a subject of controversy; in any case, it isn't simple. Certainly, the unregulated slaughter by the commercial market hunters must take a large share of the blame.

But not all of it. It seems likely that with the loss of the great virgin forests — the habitat that fed, sheltered and protected them to some extent — their demise was inevitable sooner or later. Some have conjectured that it was their dense flocks that kept the population viable. Without them, the species was psychologically incapable of breeding successfully.

In any case, the last passenger pigeon died at the Cincinnati Zoological Garden on September 1, 1914.

LAKE MICHIGAN'S TREASURE ISLAND

On a Sunday morning in September, 1905, two strangers stepped off the train at Northport, a small village near the tip of Michigan's "Little Finger" peninsula.

Strangers were a rarity there, and it wasn't long before almost everybody in town had seen or heard about them.

They were elderly men, dressed rather poorly, and their only luggage was a small handbag. One was tall and thin, with keen blue eyes and a long grey beard. The other was short and heavy set, perhaps a little younger, with a foreign accent, probably Norwegian. The short man called his companion "Captain" and was addressed by him as "Mate."

From this, and from what was perceived by some to be a "rolling" gait, it was deduced that they were seafaring men.

Very little else could be guessed about them, for they were singularly close-mouthed, saying only that they were looking after resort property.

But when it was learned their destination was North Fox Island, the whole town started buzzing.

North Fox Island! Shades of Black Dog and Billy Bones! They must be after the buried treasure!

People in and around Northport had been talking about the treasure nearly 40 years. There were three different versions of the story. One was that James Strang, the Mormon "king" of Beaver Island, buried a large sum of money there.

Another story had it that lake pirates and robbers had hidden the treasure there—a chest of Spanish gold pieces sealed in fruit jars.

But the story most people believed was this:

In the late 1860s or early 1870s—some placing the date about the time of the Great Chicago Fire—a great robbery was commited in that city by two men. The treasure was $150,000 in gold coin.

Closely pursued by the police, the pair rented a small schooner navigated by three sailors, and set sail north. Several days later they sighted the Fox Islands, then uninhabited.

Still fearful of pursuit, they went ashore on North Fox, seemingly the wilder of the two islands. After dark the treasure was taken ashore in a yawl and buried on the beach above the high water mark. The spot was marked by a marlin spike in a pine tree.

After burying the loot, the party set sail for some Canadian port. The sailors went back with their boat; the robbers stayed in Canada. One the way back, two of the three sailors drowned when the schooner ran into a gale and went down. The third was picked up but died later in a Chicago hospital of exposure.

Many years passed and one of the robbers died in a Canadian prison while serving a term for burglary committed soon after his arrival. The other drifted about in the Canadian provinces as a fugitive from justice; he was wanted for participating in the same crime with his companion.

As more years passed, he eventually became a good citizen, marrying a middle-aged Canadian widow. He was always afraid to go back to the island for the hidden money, but made a chart and kept it in a buckskin pouch he always carried. He never told anyone about the treasure, not even his wife, until he was on his deathbed, when he gave her the map and told her the story.

The widow married again and told her new husband the story, but he laughed it off as a fairy tale. The treasure chart, no longer considered of value, was put away and finally lost. The new husband forgot about the matter until his wife died.

Then, while he was making a steamer trip from Mackinaw to Traverse City, the Foxes were sighted. The name brought back the story and he reeled it off to the sailors as a good yarn.

So much for the stories. In the early 1900s many old-timers in Northport believed the treasure was still buried on North Fox Island and a diligent search would reveal it.

Over the years so many had dug for it that the shores of the island began to look like God's Little Acre, with excavations and mounds everywhere along the beaches, some of them recent and some grass-grown.

North and South Fox Islands lie some 20 miles northwest of the tip of Leelanau County—between the Beaver Islands and the Manitous.

Shortly after they arrived in Northport, the two strangers hired a local fisherman, Carl Schroeder, and his son, to take them to North Fox in their launch.

After a rough passage, the strangers waded ashore and were gone about five hours.

Unbeknownst to them, their movements on the island were watched the whole time by two Northport men, Joe Gagnon and Jay Spangle.

Gagnon was a fisherman who sometimes set his nets near North Fox, where he had a shanty. He was said to be familiar with every inch of the island., According to the story he told a day or two later, he and Spangle had followed the strangers to the island and kept them under observation the entire time.

In some places on the island, Gagnon said, the timber and undergrowth were so thick that a rabbit couldn't make its way through. He and Spangle watched and waited, and sometimes lay hidden within 10 feet of the strangers. At times they were able to hear all that passed between them.

Gagnon said the strangers had done no digging, but merely walked around and blazed some trees.

Several days later, after purchasing tools and supplies, the strangers made a second trip to the island in a launch owned by Gus Petander, another Northport fisherman. One the way over they helped Petander lift his nets. Petander said they freely consulted maps and charts but would say nothing about their purpose.

This time they stayed three days, and were picked up by Petander on a Thursday. That same day they boarded a train at Northport, carrying the handbag and a gunnysack, and departed.

Shortly before the train arrived in Traverse City, a message was received from Northport advising the chief of police to apprehend the two men, "as their actions were suspicious." Chief C. W. Ashton met the train, but since there were no warrants nor any other advice from the Northport officers, he was powerless to take any action.

Meanwhile, at Northport the story had come out that the strangers had found the treasure. An employee of Petander said the two had located 13 stones in a heap on the island.

They removed the stones and underneath found a paper giving directions where to find a clump of five cedars; on one cedar the date "1870" was said to be blazed. They found the cedars and the weather-beaten date; and below this tree they found a chest of gold.

While the strangers waited for the train to take them to Mackinaw City, they sat with their hats pulled over their faces. When anyone entered the car, they stared intently out the window.

A local reporter, however, managed to pry some information out of them. According to his story, after much questioning they guardedly admitted making a find, but refused to say what or how much.

Asked whether they were aware a portion of the treasure belonged to the state, one said quickly, as if caught off guard, "All we have belongs to us. We paid our own expenses and it is ours, all ours."

This seemed to break the ice and one of them said that Schroeder, the Northport launch owner whom they had first employed, had tried to charge them $46 for use of his boat. They had hired him at $1 per hour but he insisted on charging them for the time they were wind-bound. They settled on $15.

That was all the reporter was able to get from them before the train left. He said their principal fear seemed to be that someone would take a snapshot of them.

And there the matter rests. The two strangers were never seen or heard from again, and probably no one ever will know whether they found a treasure or were just pulling everybody's leg.

UNCLE DAN WHIPPLE
LIVED 108 YEARS

As far as anyone knows, the undisputed record holder for longevity in the Traverse region was Uncle Dan Whipple.

Whipple was a late-comer to the area. He was 90 years old when he moved from Big Rapids to Traverse City in 1890. His life up to that time was an adventure story.

Born on March 1, 1800, he grew up on a farm near Franklinsville, N.Y. At the age of 22 he left home and struck out for the West—anticipating Horace Greeley's famous dictum by at least 20 years. He made his way on foot to Buffalo, where he caught a small schooner for Chicago, then just a small village surrounded by swamp. There were only two sailing ships on Lake Erie at that time.

After a long voyage he landed at Chicago and pushed on to the Mississippi River. There he fell in with a trapper named George Tasker and the two became good friends and companions.

During the next few years they trapped together in Iowa, Minnesota, Wyoming and the Dakotas and had many adventures, including several encounters with hostile Indians. They were captured three times, Whipple said, but somehow always managed to escape.

In 1843, Whipple joined Gen. John C. Fremont as a scout in his exploration of the Great Salt Lake region and the Columbia River valley. He and Kit Carson, chief scout for the Fremont expedition, became friends and later spent several years hunting and trapping together. During his 40 years in the West, he crossed the Rockies six times.

When the Civil War broke out in 1861, Dan joined the First Iowa Regiment at the age of 60, easily passing himself off as 20 years younger. He enlisted for the usual three months but remained in the army for the duration of the war. He fought (and miraculously escaped harm) in the battles of Wilson Creek, Shiloh, Pea Ridge and Vicksburg.

At war's end he came to Michigan and spent a few years at Big Rapids before coming to Traverse City in 1890. For several years he lived with his friend Marcus Akers at Hatches Crossing, five miles from Traverse City, and walked regularly there and back, thinking nothing of the ten-mile hike. After he reached the age of 100, he made a point of walking to town every year on his birthday.

He skipped it in 1902—had a spell of rheumatism and couldn't manage it. In 1907, friends held a party for him at the Glendenning household on North Cedar Street, and he greeted the ladies with a kiss. In 1908, someone drove him to town for another party in his honor.

One afternoon two months later he took a long walk in the fields around the house and when he returned he said he was tired. He was still living at the same house at Hatches

Crossing, but his old friend Marcus Akers was dead and Akers'daughter and her husband were living there now and taking care of him.

He ate a good supper and went to bed early. But he didn't rise when they summoned him for breakfast, and they let him sleep. He died an hour or two later, still in his sleep.

People said it was easy to remember his age since he was born in 1800.

ORDEAL AT SEA

Tuesday morning, August 5, 1941: a grey overcast day. About six o'clock, William and Pete Carlson, father and son, pull out from the harbor at Leland, Mich., into Lake Michigan. They are headed for their fishing grounds between North Manitou and South Fox islands.

The wind out of the northeast is brisk, and a fairly good sea is running—but nothing their 38-foot fishing boat *Diamond* can't handle. If all goes well, they expect to find half a ton or more of chubs in their nets. Both Will 62, and Pete 31, are veteran fishermen; they've been at it, year in and year out, for most of their lives. Will's father, Nels Carlson, had been fishing out of Leland since 1907.

The run to the fishing grounds usually takes a little more than two hours. Pete looks at his watch—7:55. Just then he smells gasoline. The gas tank is up front in the bow, and he checks there first but finds nothing wrong. Then he checks the engine and finds big trouble. Gasoline is pouring out one end of a copper gasline, which has broken off at the carburetor.

Pete yells to his father to go forward and shut off the tank. He himself reaches for the switch to turn off the engine. Before he can do so, however, it backfires and ignites the spilled gasoline on the floor.

"I went to work with the fire extinguisher," Pete said. "I was standing at the back of the cabin, and the wind was coming up in front, blowing the extinguisher fluid back on me. I thought I had the fire licked and turned around to get a breath of fresh air, when the fire burst out all around me. It was in the bottom of the boat, scattered from stem to stern."

Pete has already thrown two life preservers up on top of the cabin. He and his father now climb up there and spend nearly ten minutes taking off their boots and oilskins and tying on the life preservers. Pete reaches into the cabin for another life preserver but it is too hot to handle. Then he goes into the water with a rope, hoping to tie it to a clevis in the bottom of the boat so they'll have something to hang onto. But the rope wraps around him, pulling him down in the swift-running sea, and he has to untangle himself and let go of it.

"We swam away from the burning boat and waited," Pete said. "Another boat had come out with us and was about fifteen minutes run away. We thought he would see the smoke and come over. I found out afterwards that he was inside the cabin, lifting nets through a narrow opening in the side of the boat. He never saw the smoke."

The boat burns to the waterline and sinks. Pete and his father linger there about two hours, hoping that someone—anyone—will show up, but no one does. So finally they decide to swim to North Manitou Island, a couple of miles away.

"We swam along, talking together, planning for a new boat and deciding what we'd do," Pete said. "Then my father said his legs didn't feel so good and pretty soon he couldn't use them. I began pushing him, swimming behind him. It was about 4:30 in the afternoon when I decided to stop and take a rest. I floated, and when I looked over at him he was gasping. A wave hit him in the face. He started to shake and called to me.

"He said, 'I guess I'm about through. Tell your mother I was thinking of her.' I tried to help him but it was no use. I reached over and felt his pulse and he was dead.

"I decided to take him along with me, so I started pulling him toward the island. It was about ten o'clock that night when I finally had to stop. I was so weak I couldn't carry him any longer. I had to decide between trying to make it or going with my father. I have a wife and family. I guess I had to let him go."

Shortly after that, Pete sees the lights of Tracy Grosvenor's mail boat between him and the island. He shouts, but Grosvenor doesn't hear him.

"About then I began to feel pretty hopeless," Pete said. "I kept swimming, first on my stomach, then on my back and side. I'd rest and then swim again. During the night I began to wonder if I was ever going to make it. Then I saw a buoy for a fish net and I recognized it as one we had set out. I knew I was close.

"From then on I'd keep telling myself on each stroke: 'I'm getting closer, I'm getting closer.'"

Some time later he sees the Coast Guard boat passing between him and his father. He hails them but they don't hear. Then he hears another boat. He can see the running lights on both sides and the center light, so he knows they are coming straight at him. He starts shouting when the boat is a hundred yards away.

"They heard something and veered away. When they started to pass me about twenty yards away, I shouted with all the strength I had left and they heard me. They lifted me into the boat and right then I found out how weak I was. That's the closest I've ever been to passing out," He has been in the water for 20 hours.

The boat that found him was manned by commercial fishermen Marvin Cook and Percy Guthrie, both of Leland. It was just one of several fishing boats out searching for the missing men. It was about 4:30 Wednesday morning that they found him still paddling weakly toward North Manitou, less than two miles away.

He was blue with cold and exhaustion. They wrapped him in blankets and took him to the island, where he was given something warm to drink. Next morning they took him to Leland, where he was examined by a doctor, who found that he had suffered no lasting effects of his ordeal, but put him to bed at home for the rest of the day and night. Next morning he was almost fully recovered. The Coast Guard had joined the search early Wednesday morning, but it wasn't until two o'clock that afternoon that they discovered Will Carlson's body. He was found about six miles northeast of Maleski Point at the northeast tip of North Manitou Island—indicating the strength of the current his son had struggled against in his attempt to swim to the island. The cork preserver which Pete had made fast to him had kept the body afloat.

Pete Carlson (whose name, by the way, was Lester but everyone always called him Pete) told a friend that the hardest thing he ever had to do in his life was to turn his father's body over to float face down after he died. He did that to prevent seagulls from mutilating his father's face.

Pete, who died in 1988 at the age of 77, never went swimming again. He said he'd had enough swimming to last a lifetime.

THE TRAVERSE CITY
LIBRARY WAR

Not even a canny Scot like Andrew Carnegie could have foreseen that his gift to Traverse City would stir up so much conflict.

In January of 1902 the steel tycoon and philanthropist offered the city $20,000 to build a public library, provided that the city guarantee to appropriate at least $2,000 annually for library expenses and furnish a suitable site. On May 19 the City Council passed a resolution accepting Carnegie's offer and thanking him for his generosity.

Meanwhile, several good sites had been made available at prices ranging from $2,000 to $6,000. Millionaire lumberman Perry Hannah offered one as a gift with no strings attached. After months of deliberation, the choice narrowed down to two: Perry Hannah's parcel on Sixth Street opposite his palatial home and one owned by Dr. Edwin Ashton and W. J. Hobbs on the west side of Cass Street between State Street and the Boardman River. It was priced at $6,000.

On August 8th, the library site committee voted six to one in favor of the latter because, they said, it was more centrally located than the Hannah property. Almost immediately, a small war broke out between the advocates of each site.

Like most gang wars, this was a battle over turf. The east-siders wanted the new library in their part of the city and the west-siders wanted it in theirs, while the south-siders (who had the fewest troops) were inclined to favor the Hannah site.

The conflict grew increasingly bitter and lasted the better part of two years. Most of the actual fighting took place in the City Council chambers, only occasionally spilling over into the streets. There were heated arguments, accusations and threats, lawsuits and counter suits, and sometimes even fisticuffs. Seldom, if ever, has the city been torn by such internal strife.

At one point, trying to calm the waters, Mayor John Santo suggested that Carnegie's offer be rejected.

"We are a city of promise," he said. "If strife must continue, if the river which wends it way through it becomes an impassable barrier of bitterness, then better a thousand times that we return Mr. Carnegie's offer."

No one else, however, was willing to go *that* far.

The tide seemed to be turning slowly in favor of the Hannah site but opponents were still hanging in there, still throwing punches. And even after the council officially approved the Hannah site by a majority vote on May 11, 1903, they refused to back down. They hired a lawyer, Thomas Smurthwaite, to plead their case before Judge Frederick Mayne, in circuit court. He argued as follows: "The council has not the right to choose a library site, and even if the council has that right, the site offered by Hon. Perry Hannah has not been legally accepted."

That indeed was picking nits in a most egregious way, and after months of postponement and other delaying tactics, Judge Mayne threw the case out of court.

Which should have settled the matter, but didn't.

The final last-ditch skirmish was fought on March 7, 1904. The hold-outs, George Lardie and Frank Hamilton, succeeded in tabling indefinitely a motion to award the general construction contract to local builder George Lather. Nine days later, however, at a special meeting, they threw in the towel and the war was over.

Shaking hands all around, Lardie said he had no hard feelings and Hamilton, echoing St. Mark and Abraham Lincoln, declaimed, "No house can stand divided against itself." The Traverse City Evening Record told the story under the headline: "Buried the hatchet."

George Lather broke ground for the new library in May of 1904. Known now at Hannah Park, it was also the site of Traverse City's first cemetery—the graves had been moved to Oakwood Cemetery when it opened in 1861. The building was completed in 1904 and the library was officially dedicated on March 10, 1905.

Unfortunately, Perry Hannah did not live to see the completion of the new library. He died on August 16, 1904.

MY GREAT
GRANDFATHER'S WAR

Many years ago, by right of primogeniture, I inherited a small wooden box containing more than a hundred letters in fine old copperplate hand. They were neatly arranged in chronological order and tied in bundles with red satin ribbons. They were written by my great grandfather, Henry A. McConnell, to his wife Delia during the three years he served with the Union Army during the Civil War. They had been carefully preserved by my grandmother, Carrie, his only child, along with various papers, his dress uniform and his sword.

Henry McConnell joined the Tenth Minnesota volunteers at Fort Snelling in St. Paul, on August 14, 1862. He collected a bonus of $25, spent most of it on boots and gloves (which the Army didn't furnish) and sent the rest of it home to his wife. "If you need more," he wrote her, "you can get it from Pa, as I think he owes me some," Henry worked for his father in the family drygoods store in Red Wing, Minn.

Henry didn't have to go; he could have hired a substitute. And I have often wondered why he chose to leave his pretty wife, his six-year-old daughter, and a comfortable home on the bluffs overlooking the Mississippi River to go off and fight the rebs. Nothing in his letters suggests a burning desire to free the slaves or save the nation.

He was, I think, caught up in the patriotic fervor of the time. Most of his friends were joining up—it was simply the right thing to do. I suspect also that he was motivated by that age-old reason for which most young men have gone to war: for adventure, novelty, escape from the humdrum of daily living. He'd have one last fling before settling down into domesticity.

If that was the reason, it wasn't long before he realized he'd made a big mistake. Instead of going south to fight the Rebels, as he had expected, the Tenth Minnesota was ordered to join General Henry Sibley's campaign against the Santee Sioux.

In the summer of 1862, the Minnesota Sioux had gone on the warpath under Chief Little Crow. Cheated of their lands and annuities, and nearly on the point of starvation, they attacked the U.S. Indian Agencies on the Minnesota River, killing a number of soldiers and traders, and plundering the stores they believed rightfully belonged to them. They had also burned out and killed several hundred white settlers along the Minnesota River Valley, their traditional homeland.

Sibley was a former trader who had done his share of cheating the Indians. He was appointed by Governor Alexander Ramsay to capture or destroy the renegades. After several indecisive engagements in which the Indians gave as good as they got. Sibley tricked the tribe into surrendering. He imprisoned the Santee braves in a stockade built for that purpose, and after a drumhead trial more than half of them, 303 were sentenced to hanging. They were taken under guard to Mankato, Minn., for execution.

Before that could take place, however, President Abraham Lincoln granted clemency to all but 39; and one other was spared at the last minute. Little Crow escaped capture. Having no faith in Sibley's word, however, he and two other chiefs, Shakopee and Medicine Bottle, had taken small bands to the Dakota Territory and thence to Canada.

Henry McConnell was a witness to the hanging. His company was one of several chosen from the Tenth Regiment to stand guard against the threat of a lynch mob. In a letter dated December 28, 1863, he commented on this sorry affair.

"The hanging went off to a charm — no disturbance whatever. I stood within 20 feet of the gallows when the drop fell. I believe it was the biggest hanging that ever took place on this continent."

If that sounds callous—and of course it does—it should be remembered that the Indians, and renegade Indians in particular, were regarded by many people in those days as a subhuman species, little different from animals. Many white Minnesotans had lost relatives and friends in the Indian uprisings, and feelings against Indians ran so high that most were angered by Lincoln's merciful intercession.

It was reported in the spring of 1863 that Little Crow and his men had returned to the Dakota Territory and were bent on stirring up the Plains Indians to join them in a general war against the whites. Sibley was ordered to mount another expedition against them. The Tenth Regiment joined the Sixth and Seventh at Camp Pope on the Minnesota River, where the expeditionary force assembled in early June.

McConnell wrote soon after his arrival there: "We are just beginning to see something of a soldier's life, sleeping on the ground and eating hard crackers and pork, and they taste good, too."

The expedition departed for the Dakota country on June 16, trailing a line of 300 supply wagons and a herd of beef. Their route took them past grim reminders of the previous year's "Indian troubles": burnt out farms and the old battlefields at Wood Lake and Birch Coulee.

"Today we passed a small stream noted for the murder scene of Mr. Higgins, a man employed by the government to teach agriculture to the Indians," McConnell wrote. "He was shot close to home as he was returning from his fields, and his wife and two children were taken prisoner. Mrs. Higgins had the agony of seeing her youngest child killed by the very Indians she and her husband had labored to educate and enlighten."

By late June the expedition had reached Big Stone Lake without encountering a single hostile Indian. On the shore of the lake they found the remnants of Chief Standing Buffalo's village, including some wooden buildings (which they tore down for firewood) and a few recent graves.

"This is the manner in which they bury their dead," McConnell wrote. "A scaffold is built of poles and the dead are laid on them to dry and decompose. Some of the men had the satisfaction of knocking them down and using the bodies rather roughly. General Sibley issued an order prohibiting any further molestation of Indian graves."

From Big Stone Lake the expedition headed north to the Cheyenne River. It was now July and the march was blistering hot. Great cracks appeared in the sun-baked earth. At most of the camps the men had to dig wells in the dry riverbeds or near stagnant ponds; the standing water was foul and brackish, causing severe dysentery. There was no firewood; buffalo chips were used for the cook fires.

They crossed the Cheyenne 50 miles west of Fort Abercrombie and headed for Devils Lake, where Little Crow and his men were said to be camped. Sibley proceeded cautiously, with scouts well in advance and outriders guarding both flanks. One day the scouts sighted three mounted Indians who took flight and escaped. That night a nervous sentry took a stray mule for a skulking Indian and shot it dead.

At Lake Jessie, 35 miles southeast of Devils Lake, two Red River half-breeds rode into camp with the information that Little Crow and his men were camped near the Missouri River; they had gone there from Devils Lake to hunt. They were said to be nearly destitute of food and ammunition.

Sibley decided to make a forced march to the Missouri, 80 miles to the west, in the hope of surprising the Indians there. He departed with the main force next day, leaving two companies from each regiment to guard the camp. Henry McConnell's Company D was one of those chosen for that duty.

A few days later, a man stumbled into camp, more dead than alive. He was Mr. Brackett, under contract to furnish fresh beef for the expedition. He had accompanied Sibley and the main body on the march to the Missouri River, driving a herd of cattle behind the supply wagons. This was his story:

On the third day of the march, he and Lieutenant Ambrose Freeman of the First Cavalry had gone hunting on horseback. They put up an antelope, gave chase and brought it down. They were joined by three of Sibley's half-breed scouts as they were engaged in dressing it out. On their way back to overtake the wagons, all five were suddenly attacked by 15 mounted Indians. The Lieutenant was shot with an arrow and died almost instantly. Brackett jumped from his horse and hid in the tall grass. He succeeded in eluding the Indians and made his way on foot to the camp at Lake Jessie, traveling mostly at night. For two days he subsisted on nothing but frogs.

"The scouts gave themselves up," wrote McConnell. "They were carried off as prisoners of war. The hostiles also took Brackett's and Freeman's horses. Brackett's limbs are so swollen he is hardly able to move."

Sibley's strike force returned to camp on August 1. All it had to show for many days of hard marching was one half starved Indian boy, Wowinapa, Little Crow's son, who had been captured near Devils Lake. Sibley's men discovered him eating the raw haunches of a wolf he had killed with his last charge of ammunition. The 16-year-old boy told the following story:

He and his father and 16 other Indians had left Devils Lake several days before and travelled on foot to their old homeland in the Minnesota River Valley. Their aim was to steal some horses. Wowinapa and his father were picking some raspberries by their hidden camp near the settlement of Hutchinson when they were fired upon by two settlers returning from a deer hunt. Little Crow was hit and died on the spot. The boy escaped and, after warning his companions, made his way back to Devils Lake, hoping to find other members of the party there.

In a letter to his wife, McConnell poured scorn on the whole sorry business: "The scene of his capture is said to have been a most brilliant and thrilling affair. Surrounded by 100 grave and determined men led on by two gallant captains, with guns ready and only awaiting the command to fire, the defenseless savage surrendered at discretion, thus depriving his undaunted captors the chance to display their gallantry and courage. (Wowinapa was taken back to Fort Snelling, tried and condemned to death. Later his sentence was commuted, and he spent several years in a Federal prison before finally being released.)

By late August the expedition was homeward bound, having scattered the remnants of the Santee Sioux and driven them across the Missouri River. Enroute, at Sauk Center, Minn., McConnell wrote his wife, "There's a stockade here and three companies of soldiers—also about *30 women,* soldiers' wives. *I tell you calico looks pretty fine.*" The emphasis is his.

In the same letter: "Oh, how I wish I could go home and stay there when this expedition is over. If I get home again I shall know how to appreciate the comforts of home and my dear wife and girl."

Henry got his wish. His regiment was given a two-week furlough when it arrived at Fort Snelling, and he was restored to the bosom of his family once again.

On October 1, orders came to report for duty at St. Louis, Mo.; and on the evening of the 5th., Henry, along with other soldiers from Red Wing, boarded the steamer *Northern Light* at Reed Landing, a few miles below his hometown. His wife and daughter were there to see him off, and there was a scene at the levee that tugged at the heartstrings. It involved my grandmother.

Henry wrote: "I was just as grieved as Carrie was at not getting another kiss before I left. I kept looking for her all over the levee and did not go aboard until the last moment. Then I saw her coming as fast as she could run, but it was too late. I felt so sorry to see her standing there crying."

The troops disembarked at Dunleith, Ill., and finished the journey to St. Louis by rail. As the largest military headquarters in the west, the city was full of soldiers. It was the duty of the Tenth Regiment to guard prisons and supply depots; also to patrol the streets at night, checking the saloons and bawdy houses for enlisted men without a pass. Henry's reaction to the big city was one of awe mixed with disapproval.

"St. Louis is a fine large city," he wrote. "I noticed several large buildings as we passed through, among which was General Freemont's house. I have not been out in the evening yet, but I hear others tell awful stories about its wickedness and corruption. I have made up my mind to keep aloof from all such evil influences."

Later he did venture out one evening to attend a popular melodrama at one of the city's theatres. He was impressed by the play but disgusted with the audience. "The scene where Mazeppa is lashed to the horse is splendid . . . No respectable women go there but whores are all over the place. They are the worst set of their kind I ever saw, chewing tobacco, smoking, drinking and using the most obscene language. I don't think I shall go there again."

Following a cold, damp winter in St. Louis, the Tenth travelled by steamer to Columbus, Ky. in the spring, where it spent a month in company and battalion drill. The boredom of this routine was relieved in May by a five-day raid to Maysville, Ky., in an unsuccessful attempt to cut off General Nathan Bedford Forrest, who was returning from a raid of his own against Paducah, Ky. This was the regiment's first brush with the legendary Forrest, whose reputation for dash and daring was second to none.

The operation was much too slow to intercept Forrest, who travelled with the wind; and perhaps out of frustration the troops laid waste the "secesh" countryside, burning and pillaging. The Tenth on this foray was accompanied by regiments from Missouri and Indiana.

Henry was appalled. "It was one of the most shameful raids ever known," he wrote. "The Missouri and Indiana men were all a set of robbers and thieves. They plundered and destroyed everything that fell into their hands, robbing people of their last mouthful of provision, breaking open closets and bureaus and stealing even children's clothing, bedding, crockery, mirrors and everything they could carry off."

By late June the regiment was again on the move, first by river to Memphis, then by rail and foot to LaGrange, Tenn., on the Memphis & Charleston Railroad. Here they joined elements of the 16th Army Corps under General A. J. Smith, for operations against Forrest, said to be in the vicinity of Corinth, Miss. with a large body of men.

The Federals had a habit of overestimating Forrest's strength. He moved with such lightning speed, hit so hard and so unexpectedly, that his reputation alone was worth a couple of regiments. Just a month before, a similar expedition had met with disaster. At Brice's Crossroads, Forrest, with half his opponent's strength, thrashed General Sam Sturgis and drove him from the field. The Federals had retreated and fled to Memphis, with Forrest slashing at their heels all the way.

Of this affair, McConnell wrote to his wife from Camp LaGrange: "700 men of the Ninth Minnesota are here—250 of them were taken prisoners or killed in the battle with Forrest. They say that Sturgis was drunk at the time and will be arrested as a traitor." Sturgis was absolved of the drinking charge, but was relieved of his command and spent the rest of the war waiting for orders that never came.

General Smith had orders from Sherman (who was now approaching Atlanta on the first leg of his famous march to the sea) to keep "that devil Forrest" off his back. Raiding Sherman's supply lines was just what Forrest had in mind. But with his own rear threatened by the Force at LaGrange, he paused at Corinth, Miss., to see what Smith was up to.

Smith marched south to Ripley on July 5 and burned it; then on to New Albany and across the Tallahatchie to Potonoc, which he cleared on July 11. There he showed his hand by marching straight east for Tupelo and by sending General Benjamin Grierson and the cavalry to tear up the rails of the Mobile & Ohio Railroad for a mile above and below the town. This move brought Forrest pelting down to head him off.

Smith was brought to bay in a strong position at Harrisburg, two miles west of Tupelo, by the combined forces of Forrest and General Stephen Lee, totaling around 8,000 "mounted cavalry." Smith had upwards of 14,000 effectives. On the afernoon of July 13, Smith beat off an attack on his rear and right flank and prepared to receive an all-out assault next day.

Early that morning the Tenth Minnesota was put in position to defend an Iowa battery by General Smith himself. "There," he said. "They may not get through; if they do you can give 'em hell." A week later McConnell wrote his wife this account of the battle:

"We camped that night in a fine position on an elevation covered with woods with an open field in our front and on both flanks. The enemy attacked at six o'clock next morning on our front and left flank, and for three hours there was an incessant rattle of musketry and cannon, volley after volley, as quick as men on both sides could load and fire.

"Finally, our men made a charge with a yell, driving the enemy from the field. The battle subsided at nine o'clock and we had quiet until evening, when their cavalry skirmished but were driven back.

"The next morning they attacked again and we had nearly as hard a battle as the day before, but with the same outcome. Our regiment was held in reserve both days to support a battery. We lay concealed under cover of a little rise, completely hidden from the Rebs. They came on in good style, and when they got within range we raised up and gave them a tremendous volley. They turned and ran and did not come back again.

He continued: "Well, now for myself, I was on the right of the regiment, on my horse most of the time and consequently more exposed. I experienced no feeling of fear though I could not help ducking my head when a bullet would whistle by; some came so near I could feel the wind as they rushed by. One cut the hair of my horse just back of the saddle.

"I finally decided to dismount as did also the colonel. I had hitched my horse to a small tree and stood leaning against it when a ball struck the base of it between my foot and a root. Afterwards I was lying on the ground when a ball struck the earth about a foot from my head, throwing dirt in my face."

Next day, after the fighting was over he rode out on the battlefield and was sickened by what he saw.

"We whipped the enemy badly but I hope I never see another battlefield. Men shot through almost every part, legs half cut off, groaning with pain — oh, it is a terrible sight. I counted 10 dead Rebels within as many rods, some killed the day before and still lying unburied in the scorching sun. The scene was perfectly heart-sickening, and I turned back thinking that a victory gained as such a price was dearly bought."

At midday on the fifteenth, General Smith was informed that most of his outfit's rations had been spoiled in the blazing Mississippi sun; therefore he decided to return to Memphis. He camped that night five miles north of Tupelo on Old Town Creek. Here another attack by Forrest was beaten off, and the army was back in Memphis on July 23.

On July 30, Smith again took the field, this time with 18,000 men, and proceeded down the Mississippi Central railroad, repairing it as he went. Emulating Sherman, the column left a 10-mile-wide corridor of destruction from Holly Springs to Oxford, which the cavalry put to the torch. As in Kentucky, McConnell was horrified by what he saw.

"The whole country where our troops have passed through is one of perfect destruction," he wrote. "It don't seem that enough was left to support one family. Chickens, hogs, garden vegetables, corn fields, and often clothing and house furniture have been destroyed or carried off by our soldiers."

He was especially upset by one incident. "A soldier, or rather a villain entered a house whose only occupants were a grey-haired old man and his daughter. The old man had been confined to bed for months. Despite the tears and entreaties of the girl, the soldier was in the act of pulling the sheets from under the sick old man when Sergeant Thompson of Company D happened along and threw him out."

With Smith temporarily halted at the Tallahatchie River, waiting for his men to build a bridge, Bedford Forrest embarked on one of his most brilliant and daring exploits. Leaving one division behind at the Tallahatchie front, he made a wide swing around Smith's right flank with 2,000 picked men and rode pell-mell for Memphis, close to 100 miles in the Federal rear. McConnell wrote his wife about it later:

"Forrest played a good joke on us this time. While

our cavalry was destroying Oxford, a courier arrived with the astounding news that Forrest had attacked Memphis. He entered the city at 3 o'clock in the morning and went straight to General Washburne's headquarters and captured all the clerks, 13 in number.

"Washburne himself barely escaped capture by retreating out a back window onto the roof and finally into Fort Pickering in his shirttail. Forrest stayed in town until about nine o'clock, taking what plunder he could carry off, and finally left with the loss of only a few of his men. On his retreat, he dashed into several camps, dealing destruction to all that came in his way. He killed and wounded about 20, thus carrying off 200 prisoners and 100 horses.

"It was one of the most daring raids in the annals of this war. There was, at the time, over 100,000 of our troops in and around the town, but still he entered and left without any serious opposition. The place was rapt in slumber, and so suddenly did he come that no alarm was given until he was in the heart of the city. They finally got some troops together to show some fight, but by this time Forrest was five miles away having his own fun among the cavalry and the 100-days men stationed on the roads around the city. Forrest beat old Smith this time for sure."

Forrest had aimed to bag two other generals besides Cadwaller C. Washburne, who was in command of the Memphis Department. One was alerted in time to make a dash for Fort Pickering, and the other wasn't in his own bed that night and so escaped capture. (Just whose bed he was in that night was the subject of much ribald speculation among the troops.)

In September, Smith's army returned to Memphis, having put most of the Rebel opposition in Mississippi out of commission, and within a few days was ordered to Missouri to help General William S. Rosencrans deal with the threatened invasion by Confederate General Sterling Price. On doctor's orders, Henry McConnell was left behind.

"I have some diarrhea though not bad," he wrote his

wife, "and in fact no special disease except a sort of general debility. He spent the next three months on light duty around the city.

Memphis was still jittery from Forrest's raid, and the garrison troops were kept on edge by frequent alarms and rumors that he was again approaching the city. On October 12, for example, Henry wrote:

"Our city is in terrible tumult. We were up in the battle at 3 o'clock and stood till after midnight. The streets of the city are all barricaded with cotton bales and every man able to carry a gun is armed — all is confusion and excitement.

"As a last resort we are to retreat to Fort Pickering if unable to hold our position, and the guns of the Fort are to be levelled at the town. If it comes to this, there will be smashing work. Fort Pickering is a strong fort and properly manned can resist an attack of 30,000 men. There are 300 mounted guns, and they can knock Memphis into a cocked hat in no time." There was no need: Forrest was far away, raiding Sherman's lines in middle Tennessee.

In mid-November, Smith's army, having failed to catch up with Price in Missouri, received orders to join General George Thomas's forces at Nashville. McConnell was directed to join his regiment there. He made the trip by river boat and went into camp with the regiment on a line of battle just south of the city.

Facing them was General John B. Hood's battered army, now reduced to some 23,000 effectives. The Union force out-numbered them at least three to one. The battle opened on December 15. On December 18, McConnell wrote:

"We have been fighting Hood's whole army since the morning of the 15th. Have had some of the most terrible fighting of this whole war. Minnesota has lost a host of brave men. The loss in our regiment, as near as can be ascertained now, is 20 enlisted men killed and over 50 wounded, and 8 officers that started on the charge were wounded — Col. Jennison severely and hardly expected to live, Captain White mortally wounded.

"Almost all of the above were killed and wounded in our charge on the enemy's line of fortification. The portion of the line we charged was a small redoubt as high as Barren Bluff [at Red Wing]. Up this hill of death our brave men went with bayonets fixed, hardly a sound being uttered until up to the very works, when with a yell they went over the top, driving the enemy in a complete rout.

"The ascent of the hill was terrific beyond description; a perfect storm of musket balls rained continuously upon us but we still pressed forward. I was among the first to enter the works, though how any man reached the top is a perfect miracle."

Two days later, in camp of Columbia, Tenn., he wrote:

"Hood's army is completely routed, and we are in pursuit. Unless he receives reinforcements I think his whole army will be captured before he can cross the Tennessee River . . . There is some hope that Colonel Jennison and Major Cook will recover, though both are severely wounded."

Jennison eventually recovered from a head wound. Cook shot through the lungs, died a few days later. Altogether the Tenth Minnesota took 77 casualties, of whom 21 were killed. Henry McConnell's D Company had three killed and three wounded.

As part of the brigade that turned the enemy's left flank on December 15, the Tenth received a special commendation from General Thomas himself. "It was the handsomest feat of arms I ever saw," Thomas said.

Nashville was the last great battle of the Civil War. After the scattering of Hood's broken army, the Tenth was transported up the Tennessee River to Eastport, Miss., where the men went into winter quarters. In February they travelled by river to New Orleans, via Paducah and Cairo, and camped on Andrew Jackson's old battlefield of the War of

1812. Here Henry "saw oranges growing for the first time in my life."

In the early spring, in preparation of an attack on Mobile, the regiment was transferred to Dauphin Island at the mouth of Mobile Bay, and two weeks later an assault was made on a part of Mobile's outer defenses known as Spanish Fort (it was built on the foundations of an old Spanish fortress). These works were easily taken, its defenders having pulled out the night before. Other troops stormed the main fortifications at Blakely and Mobile fell.

From Mobile the regiment marched north, following the Alabama River to Montgomery. Near Greenville, the Minnesotas got the news of General Lee's surrender at Appomatox; and at Montgomery they heard the news of Lincoln's assassination.

After spending three months in camp at Meridian, Miss., the regiment was ordered to return to Minnesota for mustering out. The men marched to Vicksburg, boarded steamers there and arrived at St. Paul on August 7. They marched to the state capitol building and were honored at a banquet by city and state officials. That same evening they marched to Fort Snelling, where the muster rolls were made out. They were formally discharged on August 18, 1865.

For Henry McConnell the discharge came just three years and four days after his enlistment. He had entered the Union Army as a private soldier and was discharged as second lieutenant. He was three years older, a whole lot wiser; and if it was adventure he was looking for, he'd had enough of that to last a lifetime. He spent the rest of his life with his family in the little town of Red Wing, on the Mississippi River, and died March 7, 1901, at the age of 71.

DEATH ON
THE RIVER

Logging in northern Michigan, what's left of it, goes on year-around nowadays. But in the old days it was pretty much confined to winter. Loggers needed snow and ice to skid the big logs out of the woods. This was done at first by teams of oxen, then by horses. Oxen can out-pull horses but they're awkward to work with because they can't back up. By 1860, horses had replaced oxen in the woods and on the farms in northern Michigan.

Perry Hannah and the Hannah, Lay Lumber Company of Traverse City and Chicago logged off the great pine forests along the Boardman River. They began operations in 1851 and when they went out of business in 1886, they had cut more than 400 million board feet of virgin white and red pine timber.

At the peak of its operation, Hannah, Lay & Co. had a crew of 400 men cutting timber in about 20 lumber camps. A typical camp consisted of 15 to 20 men, including a foreman stable boss, cook and choreboy. They all lived under one roof, a "shanty" with double-bunk beds, and a kitchen, which was separated from the common room by a railing. It was off-limits, except at mealtime, to all but the cook and his helper.

The lumberjacks worked from dawn till dark. Two-men crews felled the giant trees with axes and crosscut saws; others cut them into 20-foot logs; still others hauled them to skidways along the riverbanks. The work was hard and dangerous, but it had its compensations. The food in general was very good, and there was time for relaxation in the long winter evenings. This was strictly a man's world, but there was singing and even dancing sometimes to the music of fiddle and accordion: "female" partners being represented by a handkerchief tied around an arm. Many lumberjacks in later years had fond memories of the time they spent in the woods. In some ways they considered it a badge of honor.

By far the most dangerous work was done by the so-called "river-rats" or "river-hogs". They were the men who herded the logs downriver to the sawmill on the spring drives. The work was extremely dangerous—most logging injuries and fatalities occurred on the river. The men selected for that work were picked for their strength, agility and courage. They rode the big logs downstream with hobnail boots and a pike pole, herding them like cattle except that the logs were much more dangerous. The most difficult and dangerous work was breaking up log jams. This required not only strength and agility but also a kind of intuitive skill and cunning. A log jam could kill a man in the blink of an eye.

From 1858 until 1880, the boss of all the Hannah, Lay lumbercamps was a Scotsman from New Brunswick named William Rennie. He had been recruited by Perry Hannah himself, who had heard of Rennie's reputation as an expert logger and supervisor of spring drives on the Mirahichi River. Rennie was a giant of a man. He stood over six feet tall and weighed over 350 pounds; he had a 22-inch neck and a 58-inch chest. He was a strict disciplinarian, but nevertheless was on good terms with his men, who admired and respected him, and always attentive to their needs.

Rennie's best riverman was Charley Martineau, a young six-footer with nerves of steel, quick and agile as a cat.

One morning Rennie noticed that something was wrong with Charley. He was sitting very quiet and thoughtful at the breakfast table, some distance apart from the other men. That was strange. Charley was one of the most gregarious and fun-loving of all the men. Something was wrong.

Rennie sat down beside him.

"What's up, Charley?" he asked.

Charley looked up. His eyes were dark and narrow.

"Bill," he said quietly, "I've got a funny feeling. I think I'm going to get it today."

"Well, Charley," the boss said, "You better not go out today."

But Charley, a fatalist like most of the rivermen, insisted on going to work on the river that morning.

And was dead within an hour, helping to break up a jam.

It is said that John Rennie would tell and retell the story for the rest of his life, seldom without tears in his eyes. He blamed himself for not ordering Charley Martineau to stay in camp that day.

AN AUTOMOBILE
NAMED ELMER

In 1902, the weekly *Kalkaska Leader* printed the results of a school contest for the best 250-word essay on that fabulous newfangled contraption, the automobile. The winner was a little girl who wrote:

"My uncle bought an auto. He was out riding in the country when it busted going up a hill. I guess this about 25 words. The other 225 are what my uncle said while walking back to town. But they are not fit for publication."

This probably reflected the prevailing attitude of most Kalkaskians toward the new machine. They called it a "bubble-cart" (for a steamer) or "devil-cart" (for gas engine) and regarded it as a novelty worthy of attention, perhaps, but not likely to replace the horse.

That began to change, however, as more autos appeared in village streets—and particularly when it was learned that one of their fellow citizens was building an auto of his own design.

Elmer T. Johnson was his name, and he was regarded by most Kalkaskians as an inventive genius. He had brought his young family to Kalkaska in 1890, and had built the town's first machine shop, with the first metal lathe, on Main Street. With his talent and equipment Johnson could make or repair almost anything mechanical, but his main occupation was manufacturing bicycles. Over the next ten or fifteen years, he made and sold hundreds of bicycles to local people and, under contract, to Montgomery Ward. He also organized a bicycle club with hundreds of loyal members. It is said that by the turn of the century Johnson had put almost every man, woman and child in Kalkaska County on a bicycle.

The first news of Johnson's new project came, not from Johnson—who preferred to work in relative secrecy—but from the *Kalkaska Leader,* whose editor, a man with the delightful name of John Tinklepaugh, was a close friend of the gifted mechanic.

On November 8, 1902, he reported: "Elmer Johnson is building himself an auto this winter. He says his auto when completed will be, so far as he knows, the only steam powered vehicle of the kind ever built in Michigan."

Johnson was a big, solidly-built man — friendly but quiet, almost taciturn. People noted that he kept his experimental work under wraps and would immediately drop work on it whenever a visitor entered his shop. When anyone asked him about it, he said it was coming along, slow.

Tinklepaugh kept his readers informed about the work in progress with tantalizingly brief news items over the next few years. Then, on July 21, 1904, he announced that it was finished.

"Thanks to Elmer Johnson," he wrote, "we were enabled Tuesday evening to have an enjoyable spin in his new auto, it being in fact our first adventure in a so-called devil-cart.

"Of the machine itself one can say that it is the perfection of mechanism, and Johnson can well feel proud of having the necessary skill and ingenuity to produce an auto that combines strength, speed, and ease of management."

The new marvel was an open steam-driven coupe, with a leather seat for driver and one passenger perched on top of the boxed-in boiler. It had a steering wheel, hand-lever brakes, and a single cylinder, and could attain a speed of about 20 miles per hour.

This was the only steamer that Elmer built. All of the four additional cars that Elmer is known to have built had gasoline internal-combustion engines. (According to the Johnson family tradition and village legend, Johnson is supposed to have built seven cars, but only four have been accounted for.)

In December 1904, the *Leader* reported: "Elmer Johnson is planning to build two autos this winter. They are spoken for by local parties, he says."

One was for his good friend, Henry Stover, the village druggist. He finished it in 1905 or 1906. It was a snappy little red-and-black roadster, with a single-cylinder gas engine from the Cushman Motor Works at Lincoln, Nebraska. It had a rating of eight horsepower at 850 rpm's. The transmission was band-operated.

The second car, an almost exact duplicate, was built for Dr. Pearsall and finished in 1907. The doctor reportedly was delighted with it and promptly christened it "The Elmer," and the name stuck.

A year or so later, Johnson built another car for himself. It was much larger than the Elmer—a touring car big enough to accommodate his growing family. He is shown in it with his wife and four children in a snapshot taken about 1910.

One of the unique features of this car, invented by Johnson, was a self-starter: a system of belts and pulleys by which the car could be started from the driver's seat,

Johnson moved to Grand Rapids in 1925, and he died there in 1935 at the age of 72.

Of the four autos that Johnson built (or seven, if you prefer) only one survives. In 1952 an antique car collector, Lawrence Baum of Hastings, Mich., bought Henry Stover's "Elmer" from a member of the family. Baum and his son found the car in an old barn where it had been stored for years. It was covered with hay and in surprisingly good condition. They disassembled it, shipped it to Hastings, and restored it to shiny mint condition.

Baum sold the car in 1970 to Rose Haskin Ash of Fife Lake . She bequeathed it to the Kalkaska County Historical Society. The Elmer is now on permanent exhibit at the Kalkaska Historical Museum, which is housed in the old Grand Rapids & Indiana Railroad depot, built in 1920.

HENRY FORD'S
FRONTIER ISLAND

On Friday, June 8, 1917, the *Traverse City Record-Eagle* announced in banner headlines: "Henry Ford buys Marion Island for summer home."

The deal was handled by Ford's brother-in-law, Milton D. Bryant, Traverse City Ford dealer and Chamber of Commerce president. Bryant's home was at 403 Sixth Street, known as "Silk Stocking Avenue" because it was the city's most affluent residential neighborhood.

The newspaper story says that Ford has been negotiating for another island called "Mystic Island" or "Mystery Island" near Drummond Island, but had finally decided on Marion Island as the site for his summer home. (The story also says that nothing is known here about the other island, and, indeed, no island with any such name appears on maps of the Drummond Island area).

Ford bought the island from Mrs. Marion D. Fowler, who had owned it for many years and for whom the island was named. She was living in Chicago at the time of the purchase. Ford also bought Bassett Island, named for a hermit who lived there in the 1890s. Bassett is a tiny island off the northeastern end of Marion Island. It was owned by 1917 by the Northwestern Transportation Co., which operated a dancing pavilion there during the early 1900s. Bassett is a "sometime" island, depending on the water level in Grand Traverse Bay. At low levels it is a part of the big island.

The June 8 story goes on to say that "sometime next month, Mr. Ford and party will visit the new property for the first time." No record of the proposed visit appears in subsequent issues. But on Aug. 11, 1921, the newspaper reported that Ford's yacht "Sialia" had anchored at Traverse City the day before. Aboard was a party of women, including Mrs. Henry Ford, Mrs. R. Bryant and her three children, and Mrs. Louis Ives. Mrs. M. D. Bryant (Ford's sister Clara) joined them aboard, and the yacht made a stop at Marian Island but apparently no one went ashore.

On Aug. 28, 1921, Henry Ford and his family arrived at Traverse City aboard the "Sialia." They visited the Bryants in their Sixth Street home, and the whole party stopped at Marion Island and went ashore to inspect the property. This may have been the first time that Henry Ford did so.

There is a legend in the Traverse City area that Henry Ford, industrialist Harvey Firestone and inventor Thomas A Edison camped overnight several times on Marion Island. The legend is probably based on a trip the three famous men and their wives made to Traverse City in August of 1923.

On Aug. 16, a caravan of three "high-powered" cars

arrived at Traverse City at 9 o'clock in the evening, carrying the Fords, the Firestones and the Edisons. They had driven up from Detroit that day, and the "Sailia" had also arrived at Traverse City that day to meet them. The Fords and the Edisons went aboard the yacht to spend the night, but the Firestones put up at the Park Place Hotel. Edison was reported as "looking exhausted."

Apparently the party had planned to camp out on Marion Island but next day changed their plans and departed on the yacht for Escanaba. Ford explained to a reporter that "this is Mr. Edison's party and we intend to do whatever he wants." The "caravan," loaded with camping gear, went on to Frankfort to catch the Ann Arbor ferry and meet the camping party at Escanaba. From Escanaba they drove to L'Anse and camped somewhere in Lake Superior country.

The Fords made many trips here to visit the Bryants and Ford's nephew, Horace Ford, who had a home on Old Mission Peninsula. The only one on record in the newspaper was on May 17, 1924, when they were honored guests at a party at the Traverse City Golf & Country Club. The dinner was followed by a dance, and it was reported that Henry danced every dance, including the Virginia reel, the polka, and the schottische. The Fords were accompanied here by Mr. and Mrs. Sam Raymond, Miss Florence Bryant and Mr. and Mrs. Ed Bryant.

On this or some other occasion Henry Ford was given his first airplane ride by Milton Bryant, who owned his own plane.

But apparently the camping legend is just a legend. Henry Ford never camped out on Marion with or without Edison and Firestone.

Marion Island (now called Power Island) lies in Grand Traverse Bay about six miles north of Traverse City. It's about a mile long, half a mile wide and contains some 200 acres. Over the years it's had many names. On the early charts it was known as Island No. 10. Later it became Harbor Island, Eagle Island and Hog Island (because Old Mission Peninsula farmers used to leave their pigs there in the summer and fall to forage and fatten up on their own).

In 1881, Fred Hall of Ionia, Michigan, bought the island and named it after his daughter, Marion. In 1917, as already noted, she sold it to Henry Ford for a reported $100,000. Ford never developed the island. In 1940, he sold it to William R. Foote, owner of the Ford agency, Grand Traverse Auto Co., who in turn sold it to W. R. Jacobs. He logged off the virgin timber for use in making shipping skids for his machine products during World War II.

The Rennie Oil Co. of Traverse City bought the island in the 1950s and developed it into a public park and camping ground. In the 1960s it was purchased by Eugene Power of Ann Arbor and given to Grand Traverse County for the same use.

Jep Bisbee was a fiddler from Paris, Michigan, who, under Ford's sponsorship became known as the champion fiddler in the country.

Ford met Bisbee for the first time on his visit to Traverse City in May 1924. Ford picked the man up at Paris and brought him to Traverse City to play fiddle at the Country Club dance.

Later, Ford sent Bisbee to East Orange, N.J., in his private railroad car so that Thomas Edison could record his fiddle playing for posterity.

Ford loved fiddle music and played the fiddle himself on his genuine Stradivarius, valued in the 1920s at $75,000, but he never played well, and admitted it.

THE MYSTERY OF
ALBERT SMITH

One summer day in 1853 Lyman and Louisa Smith and their five children disembarked from a schooner at the tiny village of Traverse City, Mich., then only two years old. They spent the next two days hacking a trail for the wagon and livestock through the wilderness to their 40-acre homestead on Silver Lake, a distance of about eight miles.

They were the first settlers in what is now Garfield Township, Grand Traverse County, and the only white settlers between Traverse City and Newaygo. It is said that for nine months Mrs. Smith saw only two white women. A few local Indians were their only neighbors until 1859, when

William Monroe and his family homesteaded a farm near what is now Monroe Center, a few miles south.

The Smith family's sixth child, Albert, was born on the wilderness farm in 1858. On July 22, 1861, he disappeared.

After a weeks-long search of the woods for miles around and dragging the lake, which turned up no trace of the missing child, the family sadly concluded that he had been "stolen" by the Indians.

Traverse City's weekly newspaper, *Grand Traverse Herald,* told the story on August 2, 1861: "A little child of Mr. Lyman Smith was lost about ten days ago in a most unaccountable manner. He was playing about the yard of their log house while some members of the family were picking peas. After a few moments he was missed, and no traces of him have been found, though a most diligent search has been made in every direction.

"A bear has been seen in that neighborhood recently, and some suppose that the child was carried off by that animal; others that he was drowned in the lake; others that the Indians have stolen it, which is impossible. The whole affair is enveloped in mystery, and the parents are suffering from a terrible suspense."

For 35 years the mystery remained unsolved. Then, in 1895, a man who claimed to be Albert Smith showed up on the family doorstep. Like the missing boy, his hair was red, and he said his age was 38, which also squared with the known facts. Joyfully, the family took him into its bosom and welcomed him as its long-lost son and brother. Unfortunately, father Lyman Smith wasn't on hand to greet his son's homecoming; he had died in 1882.

Pressed by the family for an account of his long absence, Albert told then a fantastic story.

He said that recollections of his early boyhood were understandably dim, but he had been told by the Indians that his abductor was a disgruntled Indian chief named Whitefoot, in revenge for mistreatment by the whites. He said Whitefoot took him to Port Huron and then to Sarnia, where the chief's people were camped. After that he had spent many years travelling with several Indian tribes in the Northwest Territories and British Columbia. The life was hard, but the Indians treated him as considerately as they did their own children. Indeed, he said, he was given special care and consideration.

In 1876, he said, there was trouble between the Indians and the white settlers in Minnesota. He and the tribe that held him were camped 35 miles from Northfield, Minn. By that time, he said, he was tired of his wandering, half-starved existence, and, according to an account in the *Grand Traverse Herald,* "found means to inform the U. S. scouts where the Indians were camped."

His captors discovered his treachery and were forced to flee, he said, but before they did so, they strapped him to a wooden stake, piled wood around it and set it afire. Then they fled, "there being no time to stay and witness his dying agony."

Smith said he was rescued in the nick of time by a man named John C. James, who was leading a party of settlers to the Far West. James found the young man unconscious on the dying coals, the leather straps that bound him having been burnt off. He was "badly injured" but was nursed back to health and was able to accompany James and his party to Montana and Colorado.

In 1878, Smith's story continued, James and his wife and three children journeyed into the mountains from Denver in search of gold. Some 80 miles west of the city they were attacked by masked men and James was killed. Miraculously, Smith managed to escape with the three children and made his way on foot back to Denver. Later, a rescue party found Mrs. James dead of exposure.

Smith eventually took to herding cattle and spent 14

years, from 1882 to 1896, as a cowboy in Montana, Colorado and New Mexico.

Smith said that during his wandering with the Indians he met an old Indian woman near Winnipeg who told him that he had indeed been kidnapped from his home, and she remembered the ordeal by fire.

The *Herald* story concluded: "Albert Smith is now united with his family. The aged mother is happy with her long-lost boy, and the brothers and sisters give him glad welcome. The chain of evidence is complete and no one doubts that the 'Silver Lake Mystery' is happily solved."

But is it really?

Marguerite Homrich of Casanovia, Mich., tells a different story.

At 94, she is the oldest living member of the Smith family. She is the daughter of Lyman and Louisa's son, Frank Smith, who died at his home in Blair Township at the age of 94.

She says that the family was skeptical about "Albert" almost from the start. With the exception of mother Louisa, they came to believe that he was an imposter.

Lyman and Louisa were friendly with the local Indians. They had worked out a barter system with them. In one of their outbuildings they would leave flour, sugar and other staples, and in exchange the Indians would leave venison, fish and baskets.

On the day that Albert disappeared, the Indians left their usual offering but took nothing in return. So maybe Albert wasn't stolen after all—just exchanged.

"My father said that Albert's footprints were found on the shore of Silver Lake, and there was an Indian moccasin print next to them," Homrich says.

"Lyman died, and as Louisa was getting old, she wanted to find her son, so they put a notice in the paper searching for him. A young man showed up, but the boys were convinced he was an imposter. So they opened a letter he was sending to a friend in Grand Rapids. In it he told how he 'had it made', that he had been given two ponies and a surrey. So the boys told him to leave, which he did."

After that, the *Herald* and other Traverse City newspapers kept track of Smith's activities and whereabouts. They reveal certain things about his character and reliability.

"Albert Smith, the young man stolen by the Indians 35 years ago, will lecture on his life's history at the Salvation Army's hall on Saturday evening, Dec. 5. He will be dressed in Indian costume and also will have wigwams with him. Everybody come. Admission 15 cents, children 10 cents."—*Grand Traverse Herald,* Dec. 3, 1896.

"Albert Smith, the Indian captive, is giving an interesting lecture in the town of Antrim County to large audiences. Beginning July 1, he will carry a tent and have with him an Indian band."—*Traverse City Morning Record,* June 10, 1897.

"Albert Smith, the 'Indian Captive', has again an opportunity to come before the public, but from all accounts will not avail himself of it. His wife, Mabel C. Smith, has announced divorce proceedings against Smith, charging desertion. The couple were married in this city in 1897.

"At last accounts, Smith had written a letter stating he was soon to leave for Toronto, Ont., to secure his 'Indian money', which was advertised as awaiting him there. It is now stated that this fortune awaiting him at Toronto from an Indian agent—money left to Smith, so the story went, by the Indians who had kidnapped him as a child from near Silver Lake— was but a 'blind' to get Smith across the border without extradition papers, it being realized that Smith is wanted in the Queen's dominion for some offenses.

"Smith's present whereabouts are unknown."—*Traverse Bay Eagle,* Jan. 14, 1901.

Enough said? Anyhow, one thing now seems clear: the mystery of what really happened to Albert Smith is still a mystery.

Author's Note: According to Mrs. Homrich, members of the Smith family subsequently heard reports of a red-headed Indian chief living near Ontonagan, Mich., but apparently they were unable or unwilling to pursue the matter.

JONES' FOLLY

In the 1860s there was a lot more to Crystal Lake then there is today.

The virgin hardwood forest crowded down to the water's edge. There was hardly a stretch of sandy beach, and in most places you couldn't walk dryshod between the water and the overhanging trees.

But all that changed abruptly in 1873.

In the early 1870s, an Illinois businessman and fruit farmer named Archibald Jones bought the property of the Rev. James B. Walker in Benzonia and moved his family into the big colonial Walker house, one of the finest residences in the county.

Jones, with his long white beard, had the look of a Biblical prophet and the energy and enthusiasm to match. Soon after his arrival he conceived the idea of building a canal between Crystal Lake and the Betsie River. He believed a canal would open up a waterway for shipping lumber, tanbark and railroad toes to Frankfort and thence to booming midwest markets, and for supplying cordwood to the iron furnaces at South Frankfort (now known as Elberta).

Jones convinced other local men that great profits might be made on such a venture, and in 1872 they formed the Betsie River Improvement Co., with Jones as president.

After acquiring the necessary land between lake and river, they set about opening up the new waterway. The plan called for starting the canal on the south side of Crystal Lake, about two miles west of present-day Beulah. Here a small stream, known then and now as the "outlet channel," flowed from the lake through a broad swampy area to the Betsie River, about one mile distant.

In the summer of 1873, the company built a cook shanty and a boarding house near the ford where the outlet channel crossed the road to Frankfort and hired men wherever they could find them. They included lumberjacks and farmers with teams of horses and anybody else who could handle a shovel or an axe. So great was the excitement over the project that many men accepted their wages in company stock instead of cash.

They went quickly to work, straightening the outlet channel and clearing the timber to a width of 50 feet on each side. All this was done without the guidance of a qualified engineer or even the most basic surveyor's equipment.

Meanwhile, the company had contracted with Manistee shipbuilder John Torrence for the construction of a flat-bottom paddlewheel steamer, 12 feet wide and 40 feet long, for use on the new waterways.

The shipyard was located near Rice's Mill on Grace Road just southwest of Benzonia, where it is still in operation today, the oldest water-powered sawmill in northern Michigan. Under Torrence's supervision, the mill started turning out the toughest rock elm for timbers and planking.

Finally, on a Saturday in late September 1873, work on the canal was finished and everything was in readiness. Jones gave the word and his men began to cut through the last ridge of sand at the mouth of the outlet channel. The work was finished in about two hours and the pent-up waters of Crystal Lake were at last set free.

They started with a trickle, then a rivulet, then a stream, then a river and, finally, a raging torrent.

The soft sand at the outlet was soon washed away, the channel was deepened and widened, and a great surge of fast-moving water flooded the entire swamp bottom and plunged without a moment's hesitation straight across the Betsie River, filling the low lands for miles around with stray saw-logs and other debris. So great was the roar of the rampaging water that it could be heard distinctly at Benzonia, five miles away.

Some cattle and other farm animals were lost in the lowland pastures, but loss of human life was limited to a single man: a stranger named Peacock who tried to cross at the outlet ford alone and on foot. He was swept away and drowned, and his body was found several days later lodged in a fallen treetop. Another tragedy was narrowly averted when the Rev. Adoniram Joy, for whom Joyfield Township was named, managed by a terrific struggle to reach dry land.

According to another story, three boys launched a raft in the river a mile or so above the outlet stream and poled it downstream until they lost control in the raging waters of the flood. Their raft was knocked to pieces and they had to spend the night marooned on a small island in the turbulent waters.

On Sunday, the small steamer *Onward,* which served as a ferry across Betsie River, took on a dozen passengers and headed upstream. By this time the outlet stream was a good-sized river and the *Onward's* skipper, by skillful maneuvering, was able to take the boat up into the lake. There he took on additional passengers and made a circuit of the lake, tooting the boat's whistle triumphantly. It made the return trip successfully but with more difficulty because of sandbars, logs and other obstacles in the channel and the force of the current behind it.

The promoters of the project were delighted by the safe passage of the *Onward,* and pointed to it as proof that their plans would be successful. They were eager to put their own boat in the water, but by the time it was ready for launching, the following year, the fury of Crystal Lake's waters were spent and the once-navigable outlet channel was long since reduced to the original small meandering stream.

The company nevertheless hoped to salvage something from the mess by using the boat for commercial traffic on the river itself, but that too proved impracticable. On its maiden trip downriver to Frankfort the water was so shallow that the boat had to travel backward, using its paddlewheel to dredge out a channel.

After that humiliation it was obvious that the project was a dismal failure, and the company was dissolved. There wasn't enough money left to pay John Torrence, and he brought suit to recover his costs.

Jones hired a lawyer and put up a fight, claiming that the boat's construction was faulty, but he himself scuttled his case. In reply to a question from Torrence's attorney, he tugged with both hands on his long white beard and convulsed the whole courtroom by admitting that the only thing wrong with the boat was that "the bottom of the river was too close to the top." The boat was eventually sold for service on the Mississippi River, where it performed handsomely for many years.

From that time forward, the affair was known as "Jone's Folly," and Archibald Jones, a proud man unwilling to endure the ridicule, left town, never to return.

Although Jones and most of the other investors never

lived to see it, the failed project had a silver lining. The lowering of Crystal Lake exposed many fine sandy beaches, and it wasn't long before private cottages and summer resorts were springing up all around the lake. Around the turn of the century, the Ann Arbor railroad laid tracks for a branch line known popularly as the "Ping-Pong" along beaches that were once under water (one writer calculated that the water would have reached to the top of the seats in the passenger coaches) and special resort trains brought thousands of summer visitors to Beulah every year.

Thus "Jones' Folly" unwittingly contributed to the development of Crystal Lake as one of the state's most popular vacation areas.

DRUMMOND ISLAND

If the British Boundary Commission hadn't got drunk, Drummond Island might now belong to Canada instead of to the United States. Anyway, that's a tale told by old-timers on the island today.

After the War of 1812 a commission was set up to survey and determine the exact boundary between the United States and British Canada—particularly the mostly-water boundary from the Bay of Fundy in the East and Lake of the Woods in the West, which had never been accurately delineated. Among its directives was that the line be drawn down the middle of the Great Lakes and the middle of the main channel in the waterways between them, but that no island be split between the two countries. It took six years to finish the job.

The Commission, so the story goes, was headed by three representatives, one British and two American. They travelled together in an American schooner. The Americans soon noticed that the British commissioner, a man named Bartlett, went in for heavy drinking and dining at the end of the day. He was most affable and agreeable in the late afternoon, before he'd had too much to drink. After that he was apt to turn surly and contentious.

Things went smoothly enough until they reached Drummond Island late one day. By prior agreement, their course around the island was by the False Detour, a deep broad channel to the east of the island, between it and Cockburn Island. But no sooner had they dropped anchor off the north end of Drummond Island than Bartlett, now deep in his cups, began to protest violently. The Americans had tricked him, he declared; the proper course should have been by the Detour Passage, between Drummond Island and what is now the eastern extremity of Michigan's Upper Peninsula. The argument was long and heated. Finally, next morning, when Bartlett had regained some composure, it was decided that the Drummond Island question be left open until their return from Lake Superior. Also left open was the eventual nationality of the islands in the St. Marys River passage: St. Joseph, Sugar and Neebish. Henceforth, the American sailing master would try to time his daily runs so that they reached the most controversial places when the British Commissioner was likely to be in his mellowest mood.

Much later, on the way back, the Americans conceded St. Joseph Island without protest—though they pointed out that geographically and according to the terms of the Treaty of Ghent, it logically belonged to them. This was cheeky because the British had long maintained a fort and trading post on the island, but it served as a bargaining chip when they reached Drummond. Here they proposed that Bartlett make a similar concession and give them Drummond Island. The Commissioner, with several drams of rum under his belt, was in a pliant mood. He agreed to the proposal, instructed his draftsman to draw the line accordingly, leaned back in his chair—and promptly fell asleep.

It's a nifty little story, undoubtedly meant to illustrate the superiority of American cunning over British phlegm, and the only thing wrong with it is that it isn't true. The name of the British Commissioner was Barclay, not Bartlett. The two survey teams travelled separately, the British in the schooner *Confidance,* and the Americans in the newly constructed *Red Jacket.* Barclay left the details of the survey to his subordinates and seldom travelled with the party. The same was true of the American counterpart, Peter B. Porter. The big bone of contention was Sugar Island. It wasn't settled until 1842.

The recorded history of Drummond Island begins in 1815, when the British established a fort there. Having been forced to surrender the British fort on Mackinac Island at the close of the War of 1812, the British commander, Colonel Robert McDouall, chose Drummond Island over several alternatives as a suitable place to protect and carry on the lucrative fur trade with the Indians. McDouall named the island after General Sir Gordon Drummond, commander of the British forces in Canada.

The transfer of Mackinac Island from the British to the American forces was made on July 18, 1815. That day the Mackinac Island harbor was filled with schooners, batteaux, canoes and other boats as the Union Jack went down and the Stars-and-Stripes was raised. Most of the British civilians on Mackinac, and the Indians, moved to Drummond along with the garrison troops, leaving the island almost deserted except for the American garrison of some 300 soldiers. The British troops consisted of the Royal Newfoundland Regiment and small detachments of the Royal Navy and Engineers. Altogether several hundred people made the move to the new outpost.

The site chosen for Fort Drummond was a fairly level spot on a little bay at the southwestern side of the island, separated from the Detour channel by a narrow rocky peninsula. Here, making haste before winter overtook them, the garrison built several large barracks, commissary huts, and other smaller buildings including a blockhouse and a hospital. All were made of logs, and whitewashed. Some of the officers, including Col. McDouall, bought old houses at the long deserted fort on St. Joseph Island, dismantled them and re-erected them on Drummond for their personal use.

Near the harbor and just north of the barracks and parade grounds Captain Payne of the Royal Engineers laid out streets and platted lots for the village settlement. Over the years many houses were built there, mostly crude shelters of logs or poles with cedar bark roofing. The village was named Fort Collier in honor of the commander of the naval detachment. Altogether—including several structures for the government trading post—some 200 buildings were erected at Fort Dummond during the thirteen years of its existence.

The fort itself was of little military value. McDouall had placed a few cannon on a stone-breakwork enclosure near the blockhouse, and he planned to build a much larger fort with heavy guns on a rocky hill overlooking the Detour channel. But he seems to have been unaware that his position could easily be turned by using the equally navigable channel on the east side of the island. In any case, his superiors at Amherstburg dashed his hopes of making Drummond a "Gibraltar of the West" like Mackinac by ordering him not to spend any more money on military installations—at least not until title to the island had been established by the Boundary Commission, who began their work in 1816.

The British had suffered a major loss of face among their Indian allies with the loss of Mackinac. This was evident in the words of the Sioux chief Wabash, who visited Drummond in 1815 with 200 of his men.

"My father, what is this I see before me? A few knives

and blankets. Is this all you promised us at the beginning of the War? Where are the promises you made us at Mackinac, and sent to our villages on the Mississippi? You told us you would let the hatchet fall until the Americans were driven beyond the mountains . . . How had this come to pass?"

McDouall was hard put to make a credible response.

Life on the island was hard on the troops. The food was poor—several men died of scurvy during the winter of 1815-16—and there was little or nothing to do. There was heavy drinking among the soldiers, and several desertions. As an an-tidote to boredom, one of the later commanders imported a troup of professional actors. John Bixby, Secretary of the Boundary Commission, had this to say about it:

"The commandant sent to Detroit, 300 miles, for a small company of players into whose pockets the men joyfully poured their money. Among these strollers there was a modest and very pretty young woman, the daughter of the manager, Blanchard by name; and one or two of the officers went crazy about her, but in the midst of the excitement the commandant suddenly shipped off the whole party, and the flame went out."

Bigsby wondered at the poor quality of the food amidst such abundance of fish and game. "Pigeons and ducks at certain seasons are so plentiful that it is said (I do not vouch for the fact) that you have only to fire up the chimney and a couple of ducks will fall into the pot." (This may literally have been true during the spring migration of the passenger pigeons.)

"I dined at the officers' mess," Bigsby wrote. "A small square of highly salted beef, a fowl (perhaps two), a suet dumpling and two dishes of potatoes were both dinner and dessert. This was followed by a poor Sicilian wine. I was astonished." If this was typical of the officers' table, one wonders what the enlisted men dined on.

McDouall and his men were replaced in 1816 by a Colonel Maule and detachments of the 100th Regiment. Maule was relieved in 1818 by Major Thomas Howard and the 70th Regiment. Other officers and troops came and went, each usually of lower rank and fewer numbers. By 1822, the garrison was reduced to a single company in the command of a lieutenant. That year, word was received that Drummond Island had been awarded to the Americans, and the British faced the necessity of moving once again.

They took their time about it, and it wasn't until six years later that the final preparations were made. In November of 1828, a 30-ton brig, *Duke of Wellington,* arrived at Drummond to remove the garrison to Penetanguishene, Ontario. The ship was so small that the furniture and other personal property of the officers had to be left behind. An even smaller ship, the American schooner *Hackett,* had been chartered to assist in the move. Aboard the two vessels were seven officers, forty soldiers, fifteen women, twenty-six children, and three servants.

Duke of Wellington arrived at Penetanquishene on November 21 after a stormy passage. Aboard the *Hackett* were several soldiers and civilians, including a tavern keeper named Fraser with thirteen barrels of whiskey. The crew and the soldiers broke into the whiskey and got very drunk, and the ship was wrecked one stormy night on rocks off a small island at the southeast end of Manitoulin Island. All on board got safely ashore and eventually made their way to Penetanguishene — all, that is, except one horse which was left on the island and died there, giving the place its name, Horse Island.

During the following year, almost all of the remaining civilians on Drummond moved to Penetanguishene, travelling there in canoes, batteaux, and other small craft. After their departure, except for a few Indians who came and went, the island lay deserted for the next quarter century.

Passing by the island in 1830, on a trip to Detroit from Sault Ste. Marie aboard the steamer *Sheldon Thompson,* Calvin Colton recorded his impressions:

"A deserted village in this uninhabited region is a melancholy spectacle—resting, as it does, in such a beautiful spot. It really looked like a little paradise, peeping out upon the sea by the point of land which defends its harbor . . . I strained my eyes through the glass, as we passed by, but no human form appeared."

The only remaining inhabitants were the occupants of the little cemetery, a 100 x 150 foot plot, fenced in with squared cedar posts, that the British had laid out in 1815. It was nearly full when they left.

Another passerby, Douglass Houghton, on his way in 1831 to join Henry Schoolcraft on their historic journey to western Lake Superior, later wrote this:

"The first remarkable island at the mouth of the river is Drummond Island, remarkable as having been the resort of the British army after the surrender of Michilimackinac to the American forces. Here they erected a temporary fortification and quite a number of dwelling houses — most of which are now standing. From the water it has the appearance of a beautiful village, but it does not contain a single inhabitant."

The first white settlers to follow the British on the island were a colony of Mormons. In 1850, Daniel and Betsy Seaman came from Beaver Island to establish an outpost of James Strang's Beaver Island "Mormon Kingdom of St. James". They did even better than that, they populated the island. By the time they called it quits (Daniel died in 1863) they had produced sixteen children, who in turn gave birth to sixty-three grandchildren. Most stayed on the island and made their living by fishing, boating, lumbering and hardscrabble farming. Two other Mormon families, the Pierces and the Dotys, came to Drummond soon after the Seamans.

Later rivals of the Seaman's in prolificity were the Baileys, George and Cornelia, who arrived in 1880 at the beginning of a lumber boom on the island with their six children. They had eight more children in subsequent years. Today it is said that almost every Drummond Islander is related in some way to the Seamans or the Baileys, or to

127

both. Their multitudinous posterity inspired this anonymous
bit of verse:

> If you live on Drummond Island
> And Seaman's not your name,
> You'll likely be a Bailey—
> Or perhaps you'll find your dame
> Was a Seaman or a Bailey—
> Or her mother was the same.
> Now you may be a Fairchild
> A Gable, Church or Lowe
> But don't let that mislead you
> Because your wife is sure to know
> That her dear old Aunt Mathilda,
> Or her mother's Uncle Joe
> Was a Seaman or a Bailey
> In the days of long ago.

Lumbering on the island began in the early 1870s. In
those days logging was done by small jobbers who rafted
the big pine logs to a sawmill on Neebish Island and else-
where. The first big mill on the island was built by the Cleveland Cedar Company on a site that later became the village
of Maxton. Logs were floated down the Potagannising River
to a sawmill on the bay.

The first large-scale lumbering was done in the 1880s.
The Kreetan Lumber Company built a big sawmill on
Scammon Cove and maintained six or seven camps in the
woods. The cut began with white and Norway pine, then
cedar for railroad ties and fence posts, and finally hardwood
and pulpwood. The logs were hauled to the mill by a nar-
row-gauge railroad, remnants of which may still be seen
snaking through the second growth timber. The big Kreetan
mill burned down in 1920.

In 1905, a remarkable young Finnish widow named
Maggie J. Walz brought a colony of Finns to Scammon
Cove and formed a kind of commune there. An ardent worker
in women's rights and temperance societies, Maggie herself
was too busy to spend much time on the island, but visited
the settlement from time to time. She went on to publish a
magazine, "Naisten Lehti" (Ladies Journal) and to become

a world travelling speaker and champion of women's suffrage.

After the Russian Revolution in 1917, the colonists began to squabble over Socialist doctrine, and the commune gradually fell apart. One of its legacies, in addition to the many people of Finnish decsent, is the old Finnish cemetery near Scammon Cove.

Geographically, Drummond Island is both the westernmost of the Manitoulin Island chain and the most easterly extension of Michigan's Upper Peninsula. A steady stream of cargo ships from all over the world passes through the mile-wide Detour channel. (Ship-watching is a favorite pastime.) A small ferry makes trips at frequent intervals between Detour village and the island. Twenty-two miles long and twelve miles wide, Drummond is about the same size as St. Joseph Island, from which it is separated by beautiful Potagonnissing Bay with its myriad of tiny islands.

Geologically, Drummond is an island outcrop of a 400 million-year-old limestone reef that extends from Niagara Falls to central Minnesota. Its particular kind of limestone is called Engadine Dolomite, and it has been quarried on the island since 1853, when thousands of tons of it went into the building of the Soo Locks. The largest active dolomite quarry in the world is located at the island's western end. Owned by U. S. Steel, it provides the dolomite used in steel manufacture.

Drummond's present population is about 750, of whom about 150 live at Drummond, the island's first permanent settlement. The population doubles or triples during the summer— people have been building summer cottages on the island since the turn of the century.

Almost nothing remains of old Fort Drummond and the little village on Collier's Harbor. Their only vestiges are a few small fieldstone foundations and a pair of 20-feet-tall limestone block chimneys for the fireplaces that were used to heat the barracks and the mess hall. A dense grove of cedars has overgrown the 67-acre site. A movement in the

late 1960s to restore the Fort and the village as a State Park
historical site aroused opposition among the landowners and
came to nothing in the end. In any event, there is very little
of anything on which to base a restoration.

We began with a legend, and we will end with one.
This one has more foundation in fact.

Two soldiers, fed up with life on the island and home-
sick for England, deserted the post and set out for home on
foot across the ice and snow one midwinter day. The post
commander, in a fury, posted a reward of twenty pounds
for their capture, dead or alive. Two swift Indian runners
on snowshoes started out in pursuit. They overtook the deserters on a beach at Manitoulin Island, but bided their time
until after dark, when the two soldiers, cold and weary,
built a big fire and sat down on a log beside it to get warm.
As they dozed, the Indians crept up and tomahawked them.
Then they cut off their heads and carried them back to
Drummond in a bag of skins to claim the reward.

Now, it is said, the two headless Redcoats wander the
beaches of Manitoulin Island, searching for their heads. And
on cold dark nights you can see the blazing fire and the two
headless figures huddled up close to it, trying to keep warm.

John J. Bigsby, quoted earlier, provides some factual
basis for the yarn. In his account of life on the island in
1823, he wrote:

"During the previous summer five soldiers started early
in the morning across the strait to the American main, and
made by Indian path for Michilimackinac. On arriving there
they would be safe. The commandant sent half-a-dozen Indians after them, who in a couple of days returned with the
men's heads in a bag. The Indians knew of a short cut and
got ahead of their prey and lay in ambush behind a rock in
the track. When the soldiers came within a few feet the
Indians fired, and in the end killed every one of them."
Soon after that, Bigsby reported, an order came to the post
from Quebec, forbidding the employment of Indians in cap-
turing deserters.

ENGINE MAN

Hardly anybody these days has a good word to say for the internal combustion engine—so Maurice Hulett of Kingsley is something of a rarity. He loves gas engines.

That is to say, he loves *old* gas engines—the old-fashioned stationary kind with the big flywheel and the magneto or make-and-break coil, the kind that grandpa used, years ago, to buzz up firewood out back of the barn. The kind that goes chug-pocka-pocka, chug-pocka-pocka. Or something like that.

Mr. Hulett started collecting gas engines about ten years ago. Now he has more than a hundred of them: engines of all shapes, sizes and descriptions. They are lined up in an open field on his farm just south of Kingsley, and they occupy a good-size chunk of land, for, as Mr. Hulett says with a chuckle, "It isn't like collecting stamps or old coins. For this kind of hobby you need plenty of room."

How did he get interested in old gas engines? "Well, it goes back a long way," says Mr. Hulett, a big affable man with friendly blue eyes and a quiet sense of humor." When I was a kid there was a man named Jim Smith who owned a blacksmith shop just down the road from here. Besides blacksmithing, he ground corn for the farmers and made lath and other things. He used a big gas engine to operate his machinery and that old engine used to wake me up every morning. After breakfast I'd run down to old man Smith's and watch his engine running for hours at a time.

"It fascinated me—all kids in those days were fascinated by gasoline engines, which were fairly new then, everything before that being operated by steam. I wasn't interested in Smith's other machinery; I just loved to watch that big gas engine.

"Then, during school days it was my alarm clock. When I heard Jim Smith's engine start up, I knew it was time to get up . . . The sound of that big engine sorta got in my blood, I guess. It stayed with me, and that's one reason I started collecting gas engines."

Mr. Hulett has picked up his engines all over this part of the country—from farmers, junk dealers, old mills—wherever he could find them. Most of them have a story to tell and Mr. Hulett knows a lot about their history. He also knows the makes and the models and the dates of manufacture, even though many of the name-plates are missing.

His largest engine, a monster weighing almost three tons, comes from Omena. It was owned by a man named John Bauer, who operated a fishbox factory there years ago. One of the smallest engines was used to power an aboriginal lawn mower. In the days before wide-spread use of electricity, stationary engines were used for many purposes on the farm: buzzing wood, milking cows, separating cream and pumping water.

"Some collectors are perfectionists," says Mr. Hulett. "They will dismantle an old engine down to the last nut and bolt and then replace any part that's even the least bit defective. I'm not quite that particular. I clean them up with a wire brush, steel wool and a solvent — and plenty of elbow grease — and get them in good running order." Though Mr. Hulett keeps his collection out under the open sky, most of his engines will bang right off with a turn or two of the crank.

A few years ago Mr. Hulett and some friends who are interested in the same hobby got together and formed the Northwestern Michigan Engine and Thresher Club. They held their first outdoor show in 1968. Now there are more than 70 members, from as far away as East Jordan and Caro; and the 3rd Annual Show, held in August this year on an eighty-acre tract of land which the Club has leased near Buckley, attracted some 6,000 visitors. During the three-day show, visitors were treated to demonstrations of wood-cutting and timber-sawing, bean- and oat-threshing, corn-shelling and grinding, hay-baling and shingle-making — all done with antique machinery. Some of the other attractions, besides the scores of stationary gas engines all chugging away, were a steam bicycle; a mill that turns out long sheets of veneer from bolts of basswood; the oldest Bull tractor in the U.S.; and a 1909 Maxwell automobile, in mint condition, owned by the Club's president, Leonard Clouse of Buckley.

"More and more people are getting interested in old engines and farm machinery," says Mr. Hulett, who has been substitute mail carrier at Kingsley for 30 years and an employee at the State Hospital for 18. "There are dozens of clubs like ours all over the country. We have our own national magazine — the *Gas Engine,* published in Pennsylvania.

"I guess it's a kind of nostalgia. In troubled times people are turning to the old things. But it isn't just the older folks — even the kids are interested. We had a lot of them at the Show and they got a big kick out of it." He grins. "Of course the kids like those newfangled, souped-up, gas-gulping, super-duper auto engines, too."

But with Mr. Hulett of Kingsley, hobbyist extraordinary, it's no contest. He obviously prefers the old-fashioned kind, the stationary engine with the big flywheel, the kind — you know — that goes chug-pocketa-pocketa, chug-pocketa-pocketa. Or something like that.

THE BATTLE
OF MANTON

B ack in the days when George Armstrong Custer was waging war against the Plains Indians, three tiny northern Michigan communities fought a bitter war of their own. It became known in history as the Courthouse War and it lasted 10 long years.

Although no one was killed and casualties were limited to broken bones and cracked skulls, the War was notable for its alarms and excursions, marching and countermarching, feints and surprise attacks—and at least one pitched battle that mixed whiskey and petty politics in a manner that would have made the Marx brothers proud.

When Wexford County was organized in 1869, the

little village of Sherman was chosen as the county seat. That was because Sherman and environs was where most of the people in the county lived. It lay astride the first road into the area, the Northport-Newaygo State Road, completed in 1864 with the building of a bridge across the Manistee River at Sherman.

But in 1871 the first railroad — the Grand Rapids & Indiana — reached Cadillac (then called Clam Lake) and the population of the county began to shift east to the villages, Cadillac and Manton, that had sprung up along the new railroad. The people of Sherman and the western townships worried about this.

And in an effort to consolidate their hold on the county seat they erected a beautiful new courthouse in 1872.

The War began that same year when the Clam Lake faction proposed moving the county seat from Sherman to Clam Lake. It was led by George Mitchell, the powerful lumber baron and founder of Clam Lake, and what George Mitchell wanted, George Mitchell usually got. However, the proposal was defeated by the Sherman people and their allies at a meeting of the board of supervisors.

Not daunted, Mitchell continued to press his attack by every possible means, fair or foul. The bitter and prolonged contest was marked by shifting feuds and alliances, stolen ballot boxes, the kidnapping and bribing of supervisors, and board meetings that ended in fistfights.

One such meeting took place at Sherman in the winter of 1877, lasting three days filled with stormy and acrimonious debate. The Clam Lake people were so confident of victory that a large delegation, headed by Mitchell, turned up at Sherman on January 9 to watch the fun.

But one of the supervisors, Wilson Odell, whom Mitchell had bribed, double-crossed him and voted with the Sherman faction. And so the proposal to change the county seat to Clam Lake failed to get the two-thirds majority necessary to put it up for general election.

When the vote was announced on the evening of January 11, a great shout went up from the Sherman people gathered outside. They had won a victory—temporarily—over the enemies.

Mitchell died in 1878, but other equally resolute men took his place, notably attorney Silas Fallas and Bryon Ballou, later mayor of Cadillac. Ballou became the target of much vilification by his opponents because he had advocated the legalization of prostitution in Cadillac. (His motives were innocent enough: with thirty-odd bawdy houses in town he wanted to gain some measure of control over a bad situation.)

In 1881, employing a divide-and-conquer strategy, the Cadillac faction succeeded in getting the county seat moved to Manton. And in the following year, as the result of a special plebiscite held in April 1882, it was finally moved to Cadillac.

That evening, after the votes had been counted, Cadillac staged a big celebration, with bonfires, brass bands and victory parties. But the Manton people swore they'd been double-crossed and were fighting mad; they threatened legal action.

Cadillac moved fast to forestall that possibility. Early next morning Cadillac Sheriff Dunham and 20 deputized men boarded a special GR&I train of flatcars and embarked for Manton to seize the courthouse records and remove them to Cadillac. The train rolled quietly into town and stopped 50 feet from the courthouse. The doors were opened by County Clerk T.J. Thorpe, a Cadillac "fifth columnist" who had just recently moved to Manton. Within half an hour the sheriff and his men had loaded the county records and most of the courthouse furniture aboard the train.

They had trouble, though, with the big safe from the county treasurer's office. While they were struggling with that, a crowd of Manton men had assembled and were threatening them with great bodily harm; they also overturned the safe. And so, discretion being the better part of valor, the sheriff and his deputies beat a dignified retreat and departed for Cadillac.

Their arrival was met with great jubilation. However, when it was learned that the mission was only half accomplished, another "expeditionary force" was quickly assembled. Described by Judge Holden Green, a contemporary historian, as the "First Volunteer Regiment, Cadillac Militia," it consisted of the sheriff and his deputies, various town officials, half of Main Street and several hundred mill hands from the Cobbs, Mitchell, McCoy and Avers mills — some 300 men in all. They were accompanied by the Marks Comedy Company Band, a traveling troupe which happened to be in town at the time. Refreshments consisted of a barrel of whiskey and any number of private bottles.

The mood was tipsily good natured. But the sheriff had armed his deputies and some of the more sober men with 50 repeating rifles, and others brandished clubs, poles, crowbars and axe handles. Undertaker John Turner, a well known souse, carried a broom.

What happened when they arrived at Manton depends upon who is telling the story. According to the Cadillac version, they were met by a mob of every able-bodied Manton citizen and most of the farmers from miles around. The Manton people claimed that they made a dignified stand at the courthouse door only to be overwhelmed by a frenzied mob of more than 500 men, led by a drunken clerk and sheriff, who beat up everybody in sight and demolished the courthouse.

It is difficult now to sort out the fact from the fiction. Certainly the courthouse was broken into with axes and the safe removed. Blows were struck. Heads and bones were broken. Two Manton men suffered serious injuries. But no shots were fired and nobody died. And, with the Battle of Manton, the 10-year-old Courthouse War came to an end.

The story of the Battle got national attention. Cadillac

had already acquired an unsavory reputation as a sinful, brawling lumber town, and the newspapers laid it on thick. The *Detroit Post* called it "the wickedest place in the midwest." The *Cleveland News* described it as a "haven of harlots and saloonkeepers." And the *Detroit News* weighed in by calling Cadillac "the nearest thing to Sodom and Gomorrah since the original."

Over the years a body of legend has grown up around the event. One story has it that a Manton man was buried after the battle with an axe still embedded in his back. Another is that the women of Manton, before the second invasion, sallied south on the railroad and greased the tracks with butter and lard so the engine would spin its wheels.

One of the best stories is authentic. Undertaker John Turner came back to Cadillac with only half a broom. He claimed it was broken in the battle and put in a claim for damages to the board of supervisors. And the board honored his claim and granted him 30 cents to buy a new broom, thus disproving the popular belief that county supervisors have no sense of humor.

MICHIGAN'S MYSTERY
FISH — GRAYLING

Around 1850, when loggers first started cutting down the great pine forests of northern Michigan, they found the rivers and streams teeming with a strange new game fish.

It was a mystery to the early lumberjacks, who'd never seen a fish quite like that before. They called them lumberjack whitefish, lumbercamp suckers, white trout, and Crawford County trout.

New species or not, it was soon discovered that the fish were very good to eat and ridiculously easy to catch— they'd bite on almost anything. Lumberjacks got into the habit of fishing for them on Sundays and caught them in great numbers using worms, pork rind, and almost anything else that came to mind, including bits of colored wool, cherry blossoms, and even scraps of the fish itself.

The fighting qualities of the fish were known, but it's unlikely anyone had ever tried to take them on a fly—the lumberjacks were out for food, not sport.

Stories about the fabulous fish with the game qualities of trout began to percolate out of the deep woods, eventually catching the attention of sport anglers everywhere, some of whom had already suspected the fish's true identity.

All were eager to test their skills against such a worthy opponent, but there was a major problem: how to get there. Except for a few scattered settlements along the Lake Michigan and Lake Huron shores, all of northern Michigan was still a wilderness, inhabited mainly by Native American people.

A few intrepid anglers found a way. One was J.V. LeMoyne of Chicago. In 1867, he traveled by lake steamer to Little Traverse Bay, and then by canoe through a series of lakes to the Jordan River. There he found good sport, not only with grayling but also with brook trout, sometimes taking both from the same pool and one of each on the same cast. The Jordan was one of the few Michigan rivers where both fish were found, and, significantly, one of the first to lose the grayling.

Another early angler was D. H. Fitzhugh, who took grayling on the Rifle River in 1868, after riding the new Saginaw-Ludington Railroad and walking 20 miles to the stream. The logistics problem was finally solved in 1873, when an extension of the Jackson, Lansing & Saginaw Railroad pushed north and crossed the Au Sable River.

The little village on the river, first called Crawford (after the county) then Grayling (after the fish), soon became headquarters for fishing the Michigan grayling. The town lies squarely on the great divide that separates the Au Sable and Manistee watersheds. Both rivers rise from cold springs in the Otsego Lake area, and are only five or six miles apart at Grayling.

In the 1870s both were full of grayling, and nothing else in the way of gamefish—trout were unknown in these waters until much later.

Meanwhile, in 1865 or thereabouts, somebody had sent a specimen of the mystery fish in alcohol to Professor E. D. Cope of the Philadelphia Academy of Natural Sciences. He described it in the Academy Journal for 1865 as a variant of the grayling species *Thymallus,* which included other variations such as the Arctic grayling *(Thymallus areticus)* and the European grayling *(Thymallus vexillifer).* The professor named it *Thymallus tricolor,* the generic name arising from its pleasant smell of thyme when first taken from the water, the species name in reference to the fish's large, beautifully colored dorsal fin, which is not so prominent in the other variants.

The professor's findings were largely overlooked by the sport-fishing community. But the coming of the railroad brought first a trickle, then a flood, of fly-rod anglers eager to wet a line in the Au Sable River. The people of Grayling were just as eager to capitalize on their newfound notoriety as the grayling capital of Michigan. A whole new cottage industry sprang up based on the fish and those who fished for it.

Despite a certain roguish whimsicality—a characteristic of the literary style of those days—nobody has written better on the Grayling-Au Sable scene than writer/sportsman Ansell Judd Northrup of Syracuse, New York. In the summer of 1879, he and a fellow lawyer friend sent a wire to M.S. Hartwick, hotel proprietor at Grayling: "Provide men and boats for two."

The two boarded the train that night in Detroit, and after an overnight stop at Bay City, were on the river next afternoon. The Au Sable River at Grayling, Northrup wrote, was about 20 feet wide and an average one foot in depth.

The now-famous Manistee-Au Sable flatboat had already been in use for at least 20 years. Northrup provides an excellent description:

"We had two boats, flat-bottomed, with sides nearly perpendicular, pointed at each end, and each having a 'fish well' or watertight compartment, about one-third the length of the boat back from the bow. The box was made available for keeping fish alive in it by pulling the plugs in half a dozen holes in the bottom of the boat. The cover of the box made a comfortable seat for the fisherman facing bow-wards, while a round, old-fashioned 'eat hole' in the seat, on either side, invited him to plump in his fish in the box as fast as taken.

"The boatman, or 'poler' as he is locally known, sits or stands in the stern of the boat. Armed with a slender but tough-fibered pole, about 10 feet long and pointed at both ends with iron, he forces the boat rapidly along the shallow stream, around sharp curves, among the snags and through the rapids—or checks it in the swiftest current, to afford a cast over a promising bit of water—with consummate skill."

Northrup notes that the river had been cleared of snags and fallen trees called "sweepers." Below Grayling, the river gradually widened to 50 feet and varied in depth from six inches in the rapids to two or three feet. For the first five or six miles, there were no fish. But then, rounding a curve, one of the guides called out, "Grayling here," and slowed the boat as Northrup made his first cast.

"In a flash," the author wrote, "with a leap out of the water, the fish seized the fly before it touched the surface, and was fairly hooked with scarcely an effort of mine.

"I drew him in—he weighed only four ounces—and for the first time beheld the marvelous colors of the large dorsal fin and the pectoral fins, the silvery sides, the olive-brown back, the V-shaped black specks (where the trout has crimson spots) and the graceful taper form of the grayling."

He cast again and hooked a 10-ouncer, 1 inches long,

and played the fish up and down within 20 feet of the boat, despite the guide's urgent appeals to "land him!"

"It was a wonderful sight," Northrup continued. "The magnificent dorsal fin, erect like a warrior's plume, waved like a battle standard and glowed like a rainbow, and his shining sides flashed in the sunlight like silver."

The fishing party camped for the night at West's Landing, some 12 miles downriver from Grayling. The guides made a tent of blankets and a bed of balsam boughs, and cooked the fish for supper.

Northrup wrote: "I tried to believe that the grayling is as good to eat as the trout, but yielded only a modified assent."

Altogether, in a day and a half of fishing, Northrup caught 37 grayling, which averaged about a pound apiece. At the end of the second day the anglers and their guides were met, as prearranged, at Hay Road by a team of horses and a lumber wagon, and transported back to Grayling—men, boats, equipment, and fish. The catch was given to a dealer in Grayling for sale in Saginaw or Detroit.

Another party of five men, fishing the Au Sable at about the same time, took 950 fish in six days—and they were only one of many such groups. Northrup remarked that the Au Sable was already overfished. He ends his book on this prophetic note:

"The grayling is a simple, unsophisticated fish, not wily, but shy and timorous. He is a free-biter and is bound to disappear before the multitude of rods waved over his devoted head. The sport he affords in his capture, the taste he gratifies in the frying pan, and the allurements of the charming streams he inhabits, all conspire with his simplicity to destroy him. Could he but learn wisdom from his crimson-spotted cousin, and would the sportsman have pity on this gentle and beautiful creature, he would long live and wave his banner in the clear, cold streams of the North. But that cannot be."

The grayling thrived in the clear cold rivers and streams of northern Michigan for hundreds, perhaps thousands, of years. Yet his virtual extinction took place over the brief span of some 50 years. What happened? What did him in? Was it overfishing?

Unrestricted fishing certainly played a part, but only a small part. After all, many of the rivers and streams in northern Michigan were not overfished.

One of the biggest factors in the demise of the grayling was the brook trout. Grayling and trout don't get along. They can't co-exist very long in the same stream. So it became a question of the survival of the fittest, and the trout, a much more aggressive fish, ultimately won the battle.

The trout raised havoc by gorging themselves on the grayling spawn and fry; what eggs they missed they gobbled up as fingerlings. On the other hand, no trout spawn or fry was ever found in the stomach of a grayling. The latter fish subsisted entirely, it seems, on nymphs and flies.

Most authorities agree that the brook trout, which are native to the Upper Peninsula, migrated across the top of northern Lake Huron and into the rivers and streams of the northern Lower Peninsula sometime in the early 1800s. It was only after the Michigan Fish Commission had given up on the grayling as a lost cause that trout were intentionally introduced to the Au Sable, Manistee, and other northern Lower Peninsula rivers.

Meanwhile, heroic efforts had been made to save the grayling, including raising them from eggs in hatcheries (the fish disappeared after being planted in the rivers), importing hundreds of thousands of eggs from Montana (same result), and taking grayling live just before spawning season and keeping them in tanks at the Paris hatchery and in a nearby stream (the grayling refused to lay a single egg).

More than competition with trout or any other factor, however, logging did the most damage—and did the grayling in. Grayling spawn in one week in late March and early

April, the same time of year that the loggers began their annual spring drives. The logs, filling the rivers from bank to bank, plowed up and destroyed the shallow spawning beds and chased off the working fish.

Even more devastating were logging's long-term effects. Water was muddied with silt and contaminated with ground-up red pine bark from the logjams. Many grayling were found dead with festering gills. And the loss of the pine canopy raised the temperature of the water. Grayling need clear, almost ice-cold, and fast-running streams. Logging destroyed the fish's natural habitat.

Grayling were creatures of the pine forest. Some called them "trout of the pines." With fates intertwined, the forest and the fish were fellow travelers on the road to oblivion.

SHIPWRECKS OF THE GRAND TRAVERSE REGION

Westmoreland — Treasure Ship?

In the grand old days of shipping on Lake Michigan (roughly 1850-1920) most shipwrecks provided slim pickings for scavengers. Their cargos usually consisted of such mundane and unsalvagable items as grain, flour, salt, coal, hemlock bark and household goods. So-called treasure ships, if any, were few and far between.

One notable exception may have been the steamer *Westmoreland,* which sank off South Manitou on December 8, 1854. She carried a cargo of 28,000 bushels of oats, 322 barrels of flour—and, maybe, $100,000 in gold coins.

The steamer *Westmoreland* was built in Cleveland and launched on July 2, 1853. She was 200 feet in length and 28 feet in width. Her long narrow hull had the typical strengthening arches of many early steamers. On her final voyage she left Chicago on December 2, 1854.

After stopping at Milwaukee for firewood and additional cargo, including liquor and food supplies for Mackinac Island, she headed east for the Manitou Passage on Wednesday, December 6.

It was cold stormy weather on the Lake, and ice soon began to form on the vessel's sides, adding to her weight. On Thursday night, when the *Westmoreland* reached the south point of South Manitou Island, she had settled so low in the water from the weight of the ice that she began taking on water. Soon the boiler fires were flooded and, dead in the water, she was at the mercy of the storm.

With the assistance of some of the passengers, the crew launched the two yawl boats from the upper deck at 2 a.m. on December 8. One boat capsized in the launching and two people were lost. The others piled into the other boat, which made its way to a successful landing at the beach of Platte Bay.

According to the survivors, 17 people had drowned. Later, a rumor began to circulate that the 15 others broke into the ship's liquor cargo and died happy in the arms of Bacchus. Three crewmen went south and made their way to Manistee. The other survivors walked north to Glen Arbor and were cared for by local residents. Two female passengers spent the winter at the home of John E. Fisher there.

Later, another rumor started circulating: that the *Westmoreland* carried a fortune in gold coins. Over the years several attempts were made to salvage the treasure. One—perhaps lending some credence to the rumor—was made by tugboat captain Paul Pelkey, former Second Mate of the *Westmoreland*. In July of 1872, he announced that he had found the wreck and was making plans to recover the valuable cargo.

In August of 1874, the *Toledo Blade* reported that

Captain Pelkey was on his way to the *Westmoreland*. He later reported that he had found the vessel in good condition and that he planned to raise the entire ship. After a month of operations he reported that salvage attempt was postponed until the following season.

And there the story ends. No further mention of Pelkey appeared in contemporary newspapers. Did he find the gold and keep it secret for legal or tax reasons? It seems unlikely. With so many other people involved, a secret like that would be hard to keep very long.

Over the years, several other expeditions were made to locate the Westmoreland, but none was successful. What happened to the $100,000 in gold coins—if indeed they ever existed—seems destined to remain a mystery of the deep.

James Platt

It was getting late in the season, but Captain Turner of the three-masted, 450-ton schooner *James Platt* figured he could get in one more trip before the shipping season closed for the winter. That was a fatal mistake.

On November 18, 1875, the Platt left Bay City, Mich., for Chicago with a cargo of 3,500 barrels of salt. She was accompanied by two other schooners, *George W. Bissel* and *Emma L. Coyne*—all three ships under tow by the steam barge *Gladiator*. Towing would be faster than trying to beat north under sail against the prevailing northerly winds at this time of year.

Gladiator turned them loose on Thursday, December 25, after passing through the Straits of Mackinac into Lake Michigan, and the ships set sail and headed south. The wind was fair and the weather fine. That night, however, a fierce gale accompanied by heavy snow came howling from the southeast. Rather than face it head on, Captain Turner put about and sailed northeast, hoping to find shelter behind South Manitou Island. Then, realizing he was too far south, he changed course again and headed for Beaver Island.

The schooner, now under reefed foresail, staysail and jib, was staggering along with the rail under water half the time. The weather had now turned so cold that ice was building as each sea broke over the vessel, making it almost impossible to handle the rigging. Suddenly, out of the wind-driven snow came the lookout's cry: "Land on the lee bow!" It was South Fox Island—nemesis of many a lost ship—half a mile away. The crew tried to set the mainsail to keep her away from the breakers, but within a few minutes she struck so hard that the masts and all the sails and rigging pitched overboard.

Without any sail or rigging to cling to, the Captain and crew were now at the mercy of the storm. Great seas broke over the stricken ship from stem to stern, and everything was coated with ice. Fearing that they could not survive the night under these conditions, Captain Turner launched the yawl and placed the cook, Belma Champaigne, in it. He was attempting to clear it to leeward when the boat's painter caught him and pulled him overboard to drown. The cook was also washed away and drowned when the yawl capsized. All hands spent the night clinging to bits of rigging in the small shelter behind the forecastle — shivering, drenched to the skin, and praying for help.

Their plight was discovered on Saturday by lighthouse keeper Willis Warner and his assistants, but the storm was still raging and they were unable to come to the rescue. That evening, when the storm had somewhat abated, they launched a boat but it was capsized by the breakers. They kept a bonfire going all night to let the crew know that help was still at hand—and to try to save them if the ship went to pieces. On Sunday they were able to launch their boat and rescue the exhausted men, who had been without food and shelter for three nights and two days. The rescuers were astonished to find all six of them still alive. They were first mate Thomas O'Neil, John Cummings, John Hartney, Thomas Carey, Charles West and Edmund Larsen. They spent the night in the hospitable care of the lighthouse keeper, and were taken to Northport by the Coast Guard boat when the weather calmed—only a little worse for wear.

The *Gilcher-Ostrich* Mystery

On the night of October 28, 1892, two ships on Lake Michigan had a rendezvous with death. Did they also have a rendezvous with each other? The evidence suggests they did.

On that fateful night, the steam freighter *W.A. Gilcher* was outbound from Buffalo with a cargo of coal for Milwaukee. Her captain was Leeds H. Weeks of Vermillion, Ohio, and she carried a crew of 20, most of them from the Captain's home town. The *Gilcher* was a new ship, having been launched at Cleveland in December 1890. Said to be the largest ship ever built at Cleveland, she was 318 feet long and 41 feet wide. Oddly enough, her sister ship *Western Reserve* had foundered in Lake Superior two months earlier. She broke in two in a summer storm off Deer Park in Lake Superior.

The *Gilcher* was last seen passing through the Straits of Mackinac at 2:20 on Friday afternoon, October 28. At that time a great storm was brewing on the Lakes, and it reached gale strength around 9:00 that night. That was about the time when the *Gilcher,* if she had continued uninter-rupted on course, would have been in the vicinity of the Manitou Islands.

Meanwhile, another vessel was battling the storm in the same vicinity. She was the wooden schooner *Ostrich* of 279 tons. Traveling light, she had left Milwaukee that same morning, bound for Torch Lake, Mich., to pick up and bring back a load of hemlock lumber. Her natural course would have taken her somewhere between North Manitou and South Fox islands. Her captain, John McKay, was also her owner, and she carried a crew of seven, including a female cook.

Both vessels, *Gilcher* and *Ostrich,* vanished that night and were never seen again.

Next day, a large quantity of wreckage was sighted by a passing steamer, *Paunee*, on its way to Chicago. It included furniture, bedding, stanchions, and loose plank-ings — suggesting that the *Gilcher* might have broken in two before she went down — but it was not identifiable.

On the following day, the captain of the steamer *St. Lawrence* reported sighting wreckage near the Manitous and, a little later, the hull of a capsized wooden schooner floating bottom up, but was unable to make out her name.

On Friday, November 4, wreckage bearing the name *W. H. Gilcher* was found on shore at North Manitou. Other wreckage identified as belonging to the *Ostrich* was found not far away. Still later, a man named George Rowe, a former resident of South Fox Island, found what was identified as the midship spar of the *Gilcher,* while fishing 12 miles north of the South Fox lighthouse. He towed it to South Fox, where it was inspected by the lighthouse crew. The spar was split, which also seemed to suggest that the ship had broken in two before going down. So did a center hatch cover that was found later, split across the middle.

All hope of rescuing any survivors had now been long abandoned. In one of the major tragedies of Lake Michigan, a total of 29 people had gone down with the two ships.

Did the two ships have a rendezvous with death? Did they collide and go down together with all hands? In the cold light of the evidence it seems at least possible that their fates were intertwined. But nobody will ever know for sure.

The *Kimball* Disappeared

It's hard to imagine any significant connection between forest fires and a shipwreck. But that's what some people in Northport thought when little 40-ton schooner *Kimball* failed to return to her home berth after a trip to Manistee. They thought that the *Kimball* had been run down by a passing steamer while both were enveloped in the dense pall of smoke overhanging most of the Grand Traverse region.

Forest fires had been breaking out all over the region in that unusually warm, dry spring of 1891. Saturday, May 8, was the most trying day. The air was filled with woodsmoke and flying cinders and burned leaves that fell for many hours. At night the sky was red with flame in every direction. In Traverse City most of the land east and southeast was burned over. Fire came over the hill behind the Asylum and burned 150 cords of wood and lots of fence posts. D. H. Day lost a million feet of hardwood logs at Glen Haven. Isolated barns, houses and small shops burned down all over Grand Traverse and Leelanau counties. People prayed for rain.

The *Kimball* left Manistee for Northport on May 7, 1891, with a cargo of salt and wood shingles. On board were Captain James Stevens and Mate Charles Kehl, part owners of the boat, and William P. Wolfe, all members of prominent Northport families. Another passenger was a stranger: a young man lately from Norway, who had relatives in Suttons Bay, where he was headed.

After clearing the Manistee harbor, the little schooner sailed north for the Manitou Passage. But she sailed into oblivion —nothing was ever heard from her again.

A few days later, scattered wreckage began to wash ashore in the vicinity of Cathead Point at the northern end of the Leelanau County peninsula. Then Mate Kehl's hat floated ashore and was identified. Later, a trunk supposedly belonging to the young man from Norway also washed up on the beach. Several days later, the steam barge of the Elk Rapids Iron Works passed through a lot of wreckage and wood shingles that almost certainly came from the *Kimball*. The steamer *Williams* of Charlevoix was dispatched to search for survivors, but none was found and none of the bodies was ever recovered. The people of Northport mourned their death.

Did a passing steamer run the little schooner down? In view of the circumstances and the nature of the wreckage— plus the absence of any storms on the lake during this period —it seems the most likely explanation, although no report of any such collision was ever made. The fate of the Kimball will never be known for sure. It remains one of the mysteries of the Great Lakes.

The *Vega's* Ordeal

The terrific gale of November 28, 1905, wasn't the worst of storms on the Great Lakes but it was bad enough to sink or seriously disable 30 ships and carry 33 people to a watery grave. One was the steamship *Vega,* a bulk carrier out of Ashland, Wis., with a load of iron ore for South Chicago.

The *Vega* departed Ashland in beautiful weather that lasted 24 hours while the ship passed down the length of Lake Superior, through the Soo Locks and the Straits of Mackinac. But then, a strong wind driving tattered bits of storm cloud came up suddenly out of the southeast, reaching gale force as the ship was passing Squaw Island in the Beaver Island archipelago around 10 o'clock Tuesday night. It was accompanied by intense cold, a blinding snowstorm, and brutal waves rolling down almost the full 350-mile length of open Lake Michigan waters.

Unable to make much headway Captain A. M. Williams ordered helmsman Walter Jantzen to change course from south to a few points southeast. His aim was to seek shelter along the east shore in the lee of the Manitou Islands.

Jantzen did his best, struggling for two hours to maintain a steady course against heavy seas, driving snow, and a strong northeast drift, but it was losing battle. It reached crisis proportions when the seas smashed the pilot house window, dousing the binnacle lights and plunging the compass into darkness.

"The boat was diving and jumping all the time," Jantzen said, "and I couldn't see fifteen yards ahead. The lights were out and I yelled for lights. Two binnacle lamps were brought which lasted about two minutes, the first heavy sea putting them out of business. I then called a second time and the mate arrived and lit them again. The seas were rushing in over me, and I was drenched and benumbed. The lights went out again, and I managed to light them myself.

"The captain was on watch all night, cool and clear-headed, and he never left the deck except to go below to the hold to see how things were down there."

Jantzen said there was no panic, though the crew was stationed at the lifeboats, life preservers on, ready to launch at a moment's notice. It was evident that the ship was laboring and taking on water.

"Suddenly out of the darkness," Jantzen said, "she struck violently on some hidden rock and raised over it, then settled back halfway amidships, the ship immediately breaking in two, with the stern on the rocks and the bow well to forward. Captain Williams immediately gave orders for all to go forward and await daylight."

Jantzen said they were all drenched, cold and unprotected, but as the day broke, they saw North Fox in the darkness and realized that the land ahead, about a half mile away, was the northwest point of South Fox Island. The *Vega* now lay on the rocky bottom in about 20 feet of water, with the bow headed south and the broken stern to the southeast. The foundering occurred at 4:30 a.m. Altogether the captain and crew remained on the wreck for eight hours before the storm subsided enough for them to launch the lifeboats. They lost the first one but managed to launch the second, which carried five men to the South Fox Island beach. Several Indians had gathered there and built a huge bonfire in readiness for them.

The Indians, Lewis Ance and his family, and his son and son-in-law and their families, were the only inhabitants of the island. They returned to the wreck in the lifeboat and brought off the remainder of the crew, making three trips before all were safely landed. They spent Tuesday and Wednesday on the island and left Thursday noon for Northport in the Indian boats after a Thanksgiving dinner with their rescuers. Both the Captain and the 19 members of the crew couldn't say enough in praise of their kindness and help.

The *Vega* was 12 years old when she foundered, having been built in Cleveland in 1893. 301 feet in length and 38 in beam, she was one of 20 steel-hulled boats of the Gilchrist Transportation Co. of Cleveland, Ohio. Oddly enough, 10 of these boats were eventually wrecked and lost, suggesting perhaps that the builders of those early steel carriers were pushing the ratio of length and beam, for maximum speed and cargo space, to its limits. They all had welded seams, which failed under extreme stress and strain. The next generation of steel boats had riveted seams, giving them greater flexibility.

The *Vega's* skipper, A. M. Williams, was evidently one of those strong, silent, imperturbable kinds of men who could have played the part of Joseph Conrad's Captain MacWhirr of the *Nan-Shan* to perfection.

"Yes, we had our troubles out there," he admitted to reporters in what may have been the understatement of the year.

The *Rising Sun*

In the old days of sailing ships and steamers, the months most feared by sailors on the Great Lakes were October and November. That's when the great equinoctial storms come howling down from the northwest, lashing the waters into a frenzy. In one 20-year-period, 1878-1898, for example, almost 6,000 ships foundered with the loss of hundreds of lives in storms on the Great Lakes.

In the Grand Traverse region, the narrow Manitou Passage between North and South Manitou islands and the Leelanau County mainland served as both sanctuary and killing ground. It was not unusual in those days to see scores of ships riding out a storm in the shelter of the islands. But that narrow passage with its treacherous shoals and rocky reefs is also a ships' graveyard, littered with the bones of old schooners and steamers.

Among them is the steamer *Rising Sun,* which was stranded and eventually dashed to pieces off Pyramid Point in late October of 1917.

Christened the *Minnie M.,* she was built in 1884 at Detroit. She was a propeller boat with a wooden hull and double decks; a lower deck for cargo and a upper one with staterooms for passengers. She was 133 feet long and 20 feet wide and had a burden of almost 448 gross tons. During the next 25 years or so she sailed more or less regular routes under various owners between Cheboygan, Escanaba, and other points in northern Michigan.

In 1913 she was purchased by the House of David, a religious sect founded by an itinerate Kentucky preacher and his wife, Benjamin and Mary Purnell. The Israelites, as they were sometimes called, were distinguished by their code of celibacy, vegetarianism, unshorn beards and hair, and a belief in the imminent Second Coming of Christ, with whom the Purnells had promised their disciples a thousand years of life. (Those who had the misfortune to die in the meantime were dismissed as closet apostates unworthy of the Millenium.)

As another testament to their faith (all too familiar among similar cults these days) the disciples were obliged to turn over all their earthly possessions to the founders. With these resources the Purnells embarked on several business ventures., including a mammoth amusement park at Benton Harbor and a branch colony at High Island in the Beaver Island archipelago for the market production of lumber and vegetables. They also bought the *Minnie M*—which they renamed *Rising Sun*—for transportation to and from the island.

On the afternoon of October 29, 1917, the *Rising Sun* was lying uneasily at the High Island open-water dock, having taken aboard 1,500 bushels of potatoes, 2,000 bushels of rutabagas, 40,000 board feet of lumber, and 32 passengers and crew. A storm was brewing on the open lake and the swells were beginning to pound the steamer against the dock. Rather than risk damage to his vessel and the dock, Captain Charles Morrison gave the order to cast off, and the *Rising Sun* headed down the lake for a safe harbor somewhere on the mainland.

This meant running the dangerous Manitou Passage after dark, but the Captain was a veteran seaman with 55 years' experience on the Great Lakes: he'd been sailing them since the age of eleven. "I know my course," he said later. "I'd sailed it hundreds of times, and I believed I could put the ship safely through the Passage."

But soon after sighting the Beaver Island light, a blinding snowstorm closed in, reducing visibility to about ten feet. The Captain now faced the daunting task of navigating the Manitou Passage by dead reckoning.

"How's the heading?" he asked the mate, standing next to him in the pilot house.

"I don't know," the mate said, "I'm afraid the compass has taken a slue on us."

The Captain said that worried him a bit—they'd had trouble with the compass before—but he knew the course and timed himself, allowing for the gale. "A little later I knew that we had put the Fox Islands astern, and I figured we must be abreast of the Manitous, when all of a sudden the ship was shaken by a blow from a rock or bar. I told the mate to hold her steady, but he answered that she was swinging in a circle."

The blow had smashed the rudder shoe, allowing the rudder to drop to the bottom. It stuck there like an anchor, pinning the boat to the bottom. She swung broadside to the mountainous waves and the rocky shore, and the next big seas carried her over on her beam ends. This happened about ten o'clock that night.

The skipper gave orders to abandon ship. She carried five life boats, more than adequate to accommodate all 32 people aboard.

"I put young men in the first boat," the captain said. "She no sooner touched water than a mountain of a sea carried her high and dry on the beach. Women and children went next. I sent then second because I thought the men on shore could help them land. I saw the water lift their boat high on the crest of a breaker, and then the craft capsized, scattering its human load in all directions. Fortunately, we had taken the precaution to strap life belts on every one of them. As luck would have it, the men on shore rescued every woman and child."

The three remaining life boats safely reached the shore, and the Captain thought that every one was safe. But he was dismayed to find, after counting noses, that one was missing. "I am sixty-seven years old," he said later. "I've sailed the lakes since I was eleven, and this is my first accident. If a human being had been sacrificed, I'm afraid it would have meant the end of my voyage."

Happily, the mystery was solved next morning when by dawn's early light a man was seen in the pilot house window, waving a flag. He was an old man who had slept soundly through the whole affair. He was rescued later that morning by the Sleeping Bear Coast Guard, none the worse for wear.

The Coast Guard had been notified by a farmer named Fred Baker. He had been roused from sleep by some men from the ship who had climbed the bluff from the beach, seeking help. Baker hitched up his team and drove down a road to the beach on a wagon filled with hay. The children and one woman sick with a bad cold were loaded into the wagon box and carried up to the farmhouse where they spent the rest of the night.

The Israelites made their way to Traverse City next day and spent the night in the Pere Marquette passenger depot on Union Street, waiting for the morning train for Benton Harbor. Station agent Carroll, who entertained them part of the night, said he'd never seen such a cheerful, stoical people despite their misfortune.

No attempt was ever made to salvage the ship or its cargo. On a clear, calm day, remnants of it, including the engine, propeller hub and shaft, and the boiler may still be seen from the beach and the bluff.

Francisco Morazan

There's an old superstition among seafaring men that having a woman on board a working ship brings bad luck. But that was in the old days of sailing vessels, and this was 1960, and it probably never occurred to anyone aboard the *Francisco Morazan* that the ship consequently might be in jeopardy.

The mixed crew of twelve was a variety of nationalities—Spanish, Cuban, Greek and Honduran—half of them with criminal records. The 24-year-old Captain Eduardo Trivizas was Greek. So was his attractive, dark-haired wife and traveling companion, Anastasia, 29, who was two months pregnant with their second child. Their 16-month-old first-born was with relatives in Athens. Captain Trivizas, who had five years of sailing experience, was a recent graduate of the Greek Navy school.. The *Morazan* was his first command. Anastasia was listed on the ship's manifest as the "Captain's servant."

On Tuesday, November 29, 1960, the steel-hulled, double-bottom freighter left Chicago bound for Rotterdam, Netherlands, with a cargo of lard, canned chicken, hides and gelsenite. Of Liberian registry, the *Morazan* was 2,000 ton, 245-foot-long motorship, drawing 14 feet of water when it left Chicago. Its progress up Lake Michigan was uneventful until late afternoon, when a fierce gale with heavy snow squalls came roaring out of the northwest.

That night, blinded by snow and fog, the ship ran aground 300 feet off the southwest shore of South Manitou Island, missing the man ships' channel—the notorious Manitou Passage—by a scant 1,000 feet. The grounding tore a ten foot gash in her steel hull, and the ship settled on the rocky bottom in 12 feet of water at the bow and 18 feet at the stern. There she lay, battered all night by 50-mile-an-hour winds and 10-foot waves, her pumps working hard to remove four feet of water from her holds.

Throughout the night, the ship maintained contact with two Coast Guardsmen at the North Manitou Island Lighthouse, and with a state forester stationed on South Manitou who flashed light signals to the stranded ship. Three Coast Guard vessels were dispatched to the scene: the cutter *Sundew* from Charlevoix, the cutter *Mesquite* from Sturgeon Bay, and the icebreaker *Mackinaw* from Cheboygan. They arrived next morning. So did two helicopters and an amphibian airplane from the Traverse City Coast Guard Station. The seas were still running heavy, and there was little they could do except maintain contact. A 36-foot motor surfboat from Frankfort Coast Guard Station had made valiant efforts to reach the *Morazan* after receiving the first call for aid from the grounded vessel at 9:00 Tuesday night but were forced back by violent seas and icing conditions.

Although the seas remained too heavy all day Tuesday and Wednesday for the crew of a tugboat from Frankfort to cast a line to the *Morazan,* she did not appear to be in any immediate danger. Nevertheless, the Captain was worried. He feared that some of the big waves might lift the ship off the shoal and carry it to deeper water. In particular, he was concerned about his wife. He asked that she be removed from the ship and taken to safety.

Accordingly, on Thursday morning a Coast Guard cutter was dispatched to Charlevoix to obtain a breeches buoy, and on Friday morning Mrs. Trivizas was lifted from the wreck by helicopter and flown to Traverse City.

Tired and shaken, she told reporters that she was relieved to be off the wreck but that her first concern was for her husband. "I always travel with him," she said.

Describing the disaster, she said: "There was a big jolt when the ship ran aground in foggy and snowy weather. I was sitting in a chair in my room when it happened. The men started running around, getting their suitcases, and we thought at first that the ship was going to sink." She added that she was afraid during the two days and two nights aboard the stricken freighter while waves as high as ten feet pounded the vessel.

"I felt too bad," she said. "I spent all day long in bed." She added wryly that she wasn't much help, although she was traveling as the "captain's servant."

On Sunday, December 4, after five days on board the stranded ship, the weary crew abandoned ship on the Captain's orders and were taken aboard the icebreaker *Mackinaw* to Traverse City, where Captain Trivizas publicly praised the commanding officer and crew. "We felt deep comfort to see your vessel standing by while we were stranded and buffeted by the seas," he said. And two agents of the *Morazan were* on hand to praise the young captain himself for his steadiness in keeping the crew from panicking when it was blown off course and onto the rocky island reef.

Three days later a salvage tug from Sturgeon Bay, Wis., succeeded in pumping out the water from the two forward holds and transferring the lard and most of the canned and packaged goods to a barge. Worsening weather prevented the salvage crew from an attempt to refloat the ship.

The records showed that the *Morazan* was owned originally in Germany but was registered in Liberia and flew a Panamanian flag. But the present owners couldn't be found, and nothing was ever done about removing the ship.

She still sits there on her rocky perch, settling a bit more with each passing year. Now all that's visible above the water are parts of her bow and stern, temporary roosts for gulls and terns.

TRAVERSE CITY'S CINDERELLA

Perry Hannah, the so-called father of Traverse City, had three children, two girls and a boy. Claribel and Hattie married well-to-do men in Chicago and St. Paul, but Julius fell in love with a home-town girl.

Elsie Raff was the daughter of George W. Raff, a crusty old Civil War veteran with a bulldog jaw and a disposition to match. He was a merchant tailor; that is, he made clothing to order and also sold it ready-made. He was, nevertheless, a man of means. He built the first house on prestigious Sixth Street—just across Bohemia Street (now Locust) from where Perry Hannah would build his great mansion twelve years later. He also served as Traverse City's postmaster under the Republican administrations of Benjamin Harrison, William McKinley and Theodore Roosevelt.

All this, didn't cut any ice with Perry Hannah. He thought his son should marry someone of a higher social position than that of a merchant tailor. No doubt he had in mind an alliance with one of Chicago's first families—the Fields, Armours or McCormicks—with whom he was on friendly and equal terms. Moreover, there was said to be bad blood between the two men. Raff also opposed the marriage.

But the young people persevered, and after a long engagement they finally won their parents' consent and were married on June 30, 1896. By that time Julius was 38 and Elsie 34, an old maid by the standards of those days. The couple set up housekeeping in a charming house on Sixth Street that henceforth would be known as the "Honeymoon Cottage." It was some cottage. It had two stories, at least a dozen big rooms, and a carriage house at the rear. It had been built in 1892 by Katherine Barnes, widow of Smith Barnes, who was merchandising manager for Hannah, Lay & Company. Etched in the glass of a small window over its front doors is the legend "Esbe Cottage." "Esbe" is obviously an acronym for the initials of Smith Barnes.

Perry Hannah died in 1904. Since his wife Ann Amelia had died six years earlier, Julius inherited most of the family fortune. Perry had groomed him well for succession. Julius had worked his way up through most of the company enterprises, from lumbering and shipping to merchandising and banking. He was cashier of the Traverse City State Bank at the time of his father's death.

But Julius himself died the following year of a burst appendix. And so it came about that Elsie, the Cinderella girl whom her father-in-law had once slighted, came into the Hannah fortune.

If living long and well is the best revenge, then Elsie had a full measure of it, though the idea of revenge probably never entered her mind. Though childless, she had an interesting life. Until her late years she was active in the social life of the community. She bought one of the first automobiles in town, a Marmon, and took long trips around the country with her friends —once to Niagara Falls—when paved roads were few and auto travel was still an adventure.

She died in 1947 at the age of 85. Now she lies with her husband in the great stone mausoleum she built for him when he died—along with her father and mother, her sister Laura and Laura's husband, Charles Beers.

THE HERMIT
OF BASSETT ISLAND

Hardly a man is still alive who remembers Dick Bassett, the Hermit of Bassett Island. Yet Dick was something of a celebrity in his day, not only in Traverse City but around the country as well.

Not that Dick ever sought notoriety—far from it. Notoriety was thrust upon him.

Sometime in the 1870s or early '80s Dick homesteaded the little island, just off the north end of Marion Island, that later came to be called Bassett Island. He lived there for 25 years. (Marion Island lies in the west arm of Grand Traverse Bay, about six miles north of Traverse City.)

Not much is known about Bassett's life before he came

to Traverse City. He refused to answer any questions about his background. It wasn't that he had anything to hide, he said. He just figured it was nobody's business.

He was probably about 30 when he came to this part of the country, a Civil War veteran looking for peace and quiet.

The place he chose for his home is a "sometimes" island. Sometimes it is and sometimes it isn't, depending on the water level in the Bay. During periods of high water, lasting roughly for five or ten years, Bassett Island is separated from Marion Island by a narrow channel; while in times of low water you can walk dryshod from one island to the other. Bassett Island varies in size from two to three acres, again depending on how much of it is under water.

Like his "sometimes island" home, Dick Bassett was a special kind of hermit. Although he led a mostly solitary life, he wasn't anti-social. He welcomed visits from friends and even strangers, whom he entertained with his dry humor and wit. A well educated man, he could hold his own in almost any conversation. In short, he was a friendly kind of recluse—just so long as you didn't get nosey and pry into his past. Then he got as cold and uncommunicative as the Sphynx.

Dick fished for a living. He made a little money— enough for his modest needs—by catching and selling whitefish and lake trout. He also kept a beautiful vegetable garden and planted apple trees, some of them still standing.

Frank Buchan, a resident of Old Mission peninsula, spent two years, 1885 to 1887, on the island, fishing with Dick Bassett. It is to him we are indebted for most of the stories about "Old Dick". Marion Island down through the years has been a haven for American Bald Eagles, and there were many eagle nests on the island in Bassett's time. Dick had a pet name for a pair of them. He called the female "Old Hell Cat," and the male "Poor Him."

"You know, that she eagle reminds me of a woman I

almost married," Dick remarked while explaining how he named the birds. "She is the orneriest, cussedess, bossiest female I ever saw. She don't give that mate of hers no peace, and every time I see her I think about what I escaped.

"But take that male bird," he went on. "He's the feller I feel sorry for. He'll go out and catch a rabbit or a duck and bring it home. He no sooner lights in that big pine tree than the fight starts. Old Hell Cat will squawk and fret and cuss until he gives it to her and then he has to go out and find another. He only gets the leavings, poor feller."

Hermits have always held a certain fascination for their fellow humans. On the one hand are those who envy the hermit's life-style and wish they had the courage to emulate it. On the other are those gregarious types who can't understand how anybody would want to live like that. To most people of the Grand Traverse region, Dick was certainly something of an enigma.

Yet he clearly reveals much of his character and personality in an exchange of letters around 1890 with the editor of a 19th century periodical, *The Michigan Tradesman*.

From the Editor:

Dear Mr. Bassett:

I send you herewith a print from an engraving we made of you from a drawing executed by our designer, Miss Cora J. Cady. I think it would be a good time to publish your biography on the same plan, under the heading "Life of Dick Bassett, Told by Himself" and I suggest you send us a sketch of your life as you would like to have it read, to appear in connection with the picture. Of course, if you do not see fit to favor me in this manner, I shall be compelled to get up a sketch from such data as I can get, and unintentionally I might say some things that would not be acceptable to you.

To this thinly veiled threat, Dick replied as follows:

Dear Sir:

About three years ago you wrote me up in *The Tradesman*. Of course you thought it might make me feel proud to see my name in print, but I was not proud, far from it, for I partly foresaw the storm that was coming. I refer to the newspaper storm that followed the sketch. It was taken up and strewn broadcast over the land by the newspapers.

I was made to appear as an illicit distiller of whiskey, also a counterfeiter. Results—many people came here to stare at me and ask numerous questions. These included one detective, who, after cross-examining me, made a minute search of my home and island, going through places where he actually had to crawl on his hands and knees. If I had served him right, I would have doused him.

Last August I went back to town on a visit to my old army friends, and I will state that I was not arrested for murder or any other bad act.

Much as I regret to disappoint you, if you get a life of Dick Bassett you will have to write it yourself. If it is positively necessary that you print my picture in your paper, do so. I would suggest printing the following lines below it:

"The above is a perfect picture of old Dick, the Hermit. It is suspected that he is, or has been, closely connected with all the train robberies of the last five years in Washington, Idaho, Texas and New Mexico."

I object to any more newspaper notoriety. Give me a rest and abuse some of those fellows who are running for Congress. They like it—I don't."

In 1898 Dick Bassett surprised everybody and ruined his reputation as a hermit by moving into Traverse City for the winter and setting up a fish market on South Union Street. That year he had a dozen men fishing for him in Grand Traverse Bay.

The following year he came close to selling Bassett Island to a group in Chicago. Charles Thoren, secretary of the Chicago Yacht Club, has visited the island during the previous summer, and thought it would make ideal headquarters for the Summer Regatta. He negotiated with Dick for its purchase but the deal fell through because Dick couldn't establish a clear title.

Shortly after this, Dick committed the ultimate betrayal of all hermits and misogynists. He got married and left town for good. The happy couple settled in California.

Author's Note: Marion Island has had many names. On some of the early 19th Century charts it appears as Island No. 10. Later it was called Harbor Island, Eagle Island, and Hog Island—the latter because some Old Mission peninsula farmers used to take young pigs there in the spring and leave them until fall to forage and fatten on nuts and roots. (The practice was discontinued, it is said, because other people helped themselves to the young porkers.)

In 1881 Frederich Hall of Ionia bought the island and named it after his daughter, Marion. The name changed was officially sanctioned by the Michigan legislation — much to the annoyance of Thomas Bates, editor of the *Grand Traverse Herald,* who grumped editorially that it should have been left as Harbor Island.

In 1917, Marion Fowler sold the island for $100,000 to Henry Ford. Ford visited the island at least once, anchoring his yacht *Sedalia* in its harbor, and a rumor has persisted that he, Thomas Edison and Harvey Firestone camped on the island — but it never happened. It was then, of course, called Ford Island.

During World War II, the island was purchased by Parts Manufacturing Co. of Traverse City, and the virgin timber was logged off to supply lumber for wooden pallets. Later it was acquired by the Rennie Oil Co., also of Traverse City, and developed as a primitive camping, hiking and picnicking site, open to the public. In 1975 the island was sold to Eugene Powers of Ann Arbor, Mich., for $250,000. Powers turned it over to Grand Traverse County as a gift, to be used henceforth as a public park and outdoors recreation facility. Powers also contributed $21,000 for initial park development. In gratitude to him, the island was renamed Power Island.

But, of all its names, many people still prefer to call it Marion Island — no discredit to Eugene Powers intended.

WEXFORD
MISSED THE TRAIN

In the old days, the village of Wexford straddled the line between Wexford and Grand Traverse counties. That may have been because in 1871 the Wexford County Board of Supervisors passed a resolution outlawing the sale of all alcoholic beverages and declared war on "all those engaged in this wicked and unholy business." For a while, at least, there was no place where a thirsty man could buy a drink closer than Traverse City, 18 miles north.

The village was organized in 1872, and it was perhaps no accident that two saloons sprang up that same year or soon after, just across the Grand Traverse County line, safely out of the reach of the Carrie Nation crowd. Wexford was also called Wexford Corners because that's where corners of four townships come together: Wexford, Hanover, Grant and Mayfield.

Wexford is situated in a fairly prosperous farming community on the old Northport-Newaygo State Road, the first State road in northern Michigan. It was built in the early 1860s, closely following an old Indian trail. In the early 1870s, Wexford was the biggest village in Wexford County after Sherman, Manton and Clam Lake, which, hardly anybody now remembers, was the original name of Cadillac. Nobody at all remembers that Wexford County was originally named Wautawaubet.

The village was founded by a man named John Lennington, of whom little is known except that he built the first general store. John Foust, a farmer and coal miner from southern Ohio, was one of the first postmasters. But the village didn't really start growing until 1880, when white-bearded Dr. Dwight Connine, moved his family up from Sherman and built a larger general store and, a few years later, the first bank. Dr. Connine continued to practice medicine, the only doctor for miles around.

By 1890 Wexford also had another general store, a tin shop and blacksmith, meat market, hardware and harness shop, a Methodist Church (which was much later moved to Buckley and still holds services there), and a grade school with as many as 30 children. It still had the two saloons, of course, and some of the merchants complained that the lumberjacks and rivermen would cash their checks there, then spend what little was left after paying the bar bill on food and clothing. First things first.

Wexford had its chance to amount to something when it grew up, but missed the opportunity. That was about 1910 when Manistee lumberman Ed Buckley began to build a branch line of his Manistee & Northeastern railroad from Kaleva to Walton Junction. It seems that Buckley might have been persuaded to route the tracks through Wexford, in return for a modest quid pro quo, but most of the merchants turned him down. They feared, so it was said, that the railroad would hurt their business by making it easier for people to go out of town to do their shopping.

So the railroad passed by, a scant half mile south, and went on another half mile, where Buckley established his logging headquarters at what soon became his namesake village. Buckley grew and prospered because it was on the railroad, which eventually went on to Walton Junction and Grayling. Wexford didn't because it wasn't.

A fire, said to have started at the back of Connine's general store, wiped out most of the wooden buildings downtown in 1909; but they were soon rebuilt, of concrete block, along with some new ones. Dwight Connine's great-great granddaughter, Viola Kellogg, who was born in Wexford and has lived there all her life, says that at one time Wexford was larger than Buckley is now. Mrs. Kellogg has 19 grandchildren, 28 great-grandchildren, and one great-great grandson, many of whom still live in the Wexford area.

Wexford began to go downhill soon after the fire. The final blow came in the early 1930s when M-37 was improved from Traverse City to Buckley and Mesick, leaving Wexford in a backwash on the old State Road. By that time, Wexford was already on the verge of becoming a ghost town.

Little is left of it now except two or three old frame houses, a few mobile homes, two empty concrete-block store buildings, and Connine's bank vault encased in concrete. What once held bank notes, silver, and gold is now a repository for old hubcaps and worn-out rubber tires.

WHATEVER HAPPENED TO OVAL WOOD DISH?

One hundred years ago Oval Wood Dish were household words in Traverse City—and indeed, all over the country. Oval Wood Dish Company manufactured a variety of wooden household products, including rolling pins, chopping blocks, clothespins, and other domestic utensils. By far its most famous and best-selling item was its namesake: an oval wooden dish.

The wood dish was a thin, shallow, oval-shaped bowl that was the universal disposable container of its day. Thousands of grocery stores and meat markets across the country used it to dispense such things as butter, lard, ground meat, and an early form of margarine called catasuet. People saved the veneer-thin wooden containers for kindling to start fires in the cookstove and furnace.

The oval wood dish was invented by Seth H. Smith of Fulton County, Ohio in 1883. That same year the Oval Wood Dish Company was formed by Wauseon, Ohio businessman Henry Souders Hull and his partner J. W. Longnecker, in Ohio, OWD built its first factory in Mancelona, Mich., in 1883. It was moved to Traverse City in 1896, occupying several acres on Boardman Lake at the foot of Wellington Street. Completely rebuilt after a disastrous fire in 1896, it grew into Traverse City's largest single industry, and made its owner a millionaire. Henry Hull and Perry Hannah, the legendary lumberman who founded the City, were the richest men in town. Henry Hull's mansion on Wellington Street, Perry Hannah's on Sixth, and W. Cary's across Wellington Street from his father are the three most opulent historic houses in Traverse City today. (W. Cary preferred not to use his first name, which was William.)

OWD used a special patented machine tool to scoop out the thin wooden dishes from squared blocks of clear maple, beech, and birch. During its 24 years in Traverse City, the company cut some 21 million feet of hardwood timber and shipped a yearly average of 1,000 railroad cars filled with its products all over this country and abroad. It maintained a work force of 500, plus an additional 150 in the woods, and had an annual payroll of $200,000—well over a million in today's money. By any standard OWD was a major industry.

But it also had a major problem. By 1910 the supply of quality hardwood timber in northern lower Michigan was fast running out.

That was no surprise—except maybe how quickly it happened. As early as the turn of the century, the company had seen the handwriting on the wall and was preparing for that eventuality. It began to invest heavily in large tracts of hardwood timber in Michigan's Upper Peninsula and Canada, and it was more or less understood that eventually the plant would be relocated in the Marquette area.

But something happened in 1913 that began to change the picture. W. Cary Hull and OWD plant manager Tracy Gillis and their wives took a vacation trip through the Adirondacks in upper New York State in a brand-new Stutz Bearcat automobile. They were impressed by the natural beauty of the country, which resembled the Grand Traverse region in some ways—and particularly by the huge stands of hardwood timber in the vicinity of Tupper Lake, a small town 140 miles northeast of Utica.

They learned that little use was being made of it, and that the prices on such timberland were exceedingly attractive. Consequently, as an investment, without any thought of establishing in New York State, OWD in November of 1914 made it first purchase of timberlands in the Adirondacks. News of the purchase spread quickly through the region, and OWD was soon inundated by offers to sell from other timberland holders.

In an interview with a local historian in 1967, Gerald P. Hull—who became head of the company after his father Cary's death—recalled the circumstances: "We sent cruisers from Michigan to the Tupper Lake area to take a hasty look at the timber," he said, "and sometime in the spring or summer of 1915, we secured options on several large stands of hardwood timber. The total rounded out at 75,000 acres, which we estimated to contain somewhere around 275 million feet of hardwood timber."

With this nucleus the company decided to locate in New York State, provided it could get favorable freight rates on both incoming logs and outbound manufactured products. OWD immediately began negotiations with New York Central Railroad.

OWD wanted to locate in Utica. The railroad welcomed the business, but didn't want the company to choose Utica, where the railroad would be exposed to competition on the outbound products. They urged it to choose Tupper Lake. They could give very attractive per-car rates into Tupper Lake. But the only rate they would quote on logs from there to Utica was on a hundred pound basis. That would cost the company twice as much.

Since OWD's requirements were estimated at 4,000 cars per year, this was the determining factor in locating in Tupper Lake rather than Utica.

For Tupper Lake, the decision couldn't have come at a better time. The town had suffered an economic decline over the past 15 years and was already losing population. Its people had begun to fear that it might be headed for the same fate that overtook Brandon and Herrick, once thriving sawmill settlements, now ghost towns.

Construction on the new plant commenced in the fall of 1915 as the Traverse City plant was being phased out, and the first log went through the mill in December 1916. Built of reinforced concrete, the new factory was three times as big as the one in Traverse City and with four times its capacity. Adjacent to it, OWD built a mammoth warehouse with a spur track to the main line.

Tupper Lake's gain was Traverse City's loss. When OWD moved to Tupper Lake in 1916, it took with it at least 100 worker families, consigning Traverse City to economic doldrums that lasted until World War II. A large number of workers was also recruited from Ohio. Two new streets in Tupper Lake with houses built for OWD employees were appropriately named Michigan Avenue and Ohio Street.

OWD prospered in Tupper Lake and so did the town. A few financial problems were encountered in the early 1930s, but it continued to manufacture a limited number of wood dishes, and the addition of several new products resulted in record sales. Flat wooden spoons were introduced in 1932 and reached volume sales of 35 million by 1938. That same year it introduced "Ritefork" and "Ritespoon", which it hailed as "the only wooden spoon on the market with a bowl shaped like a metal spoon."

But storm clouds were beginning to gather not far off. In the 1950s, the explosive growth of the plastics industry—with its much cheaper and easy-to-make products—began to dominate the kitchenware market. The company spent a lot of money in 1958 modernizing the Tupper Lake plant, but it was too late — the end was already in sight.

In 1961, OWD sold its subsidiary plants at Potsdam, NY, and Quebec City. In 1964, it sold 22,000 acres of its dwindling timberland holdings to Diamond International. In May, 1964, OWD sold its Tupper Lake plant to Adirondack Plywood Corporation, and called it a day.